M000085011

PRAISE FOR

"More Than a Conqueror" by Porcia Baxter

Weaved skillfully within Porcia Baxter's poignant and powerful story is the blood red thread of redemption and grace. Full of insightful reflections of how God rescued her and brought her to this moment in her life, Porcia's story will inspire you to trust and believe that God is yet moving and working in the world to rescue the lost.

-Pastor Laurel Bunker, Dean of Campus Ministries and Campus Pastor, Bethel University

———

Porcia Baxter's memoir is a vivid reminder that even a "good girl" can be lured down the wrong path into a life consumed by drugs and alcohol. Through her personal account, Porcia demonstrates that a relationship with Jesus is the only antidote for those who cannot escape the stranglehold of addiction.

-Lisa Burkhardt Worley, Award-Winning Author and International Radio Host

Porcia's story is a gripping journey that will open your eyes to the depth of darkness that is addiction. However it also reveals just how truly powerful the Gospel really is. You will be convinced of the fact that Jesus has come to set captives free and He will not stop pursuing us until we are walking in the fullness of what it means to be more than conquerors!

-Mark Graalman, Youth Pastor of Vineyard Church Of Toledo and co-founding member of the band Sanctus Real.

———

Everyone has a story - each one is unique and different. Some are full of challenge and adversity and you might wonder, "How did they make it through?" This book will let you know there is hope and redemption. You're never too far gone from grace!

-Rob Roozeboom - Founder/President - RISE Ministries

MORE THAN A CONQUEROR

From the Death-Grip of Addiction to a Life of Purpose, Passion, and Hope

PORCIA BAXTER

YELLOWHAMMER
PUBLISHING

Copyright © 2017 by Porcia Baxter

All rights reserved.

No part of this book may be reproduced in any form or by any electronic or mechanical means, including information storage and retrieval systems, without written permission from the author, except for the use of brief quotations in a book review.

Print 13-978-0-9994938-4-7

Ebook 10-978-0-9994938-5-4

CONTENTS

FOREWORD

This is a story of change. At first this change is what no one wants to experience. Porcia changed schools, clothes, jobs, and addresses, but nothing brought her satisfaction. Despite all these changes, she never felt that she was good enough. Alcohol and drugs, like so many today, became her escape, her medicine, and her god. Changing rehab programs didn't work for her either, at first, as she sought recovery and real change.

I met Porcia during one of those rehab efforts. She looked sad, lonely and depressed. Though she believed in God she thought she belonged to the devil. Many attempts for real change only led to relapse after relapse.

Millions today are experiencing this same darkness of addiction. If you or someone you know needs addiction recovery, put this book in their hands. Porcia's story is a page-turner. It is proof that no matter how far from the Father's House one goes redemption is possible. Her testimony reminds me of the Bible verse that says, "Though he fall, he shall not be utterly cast down." More Than a Conqueror includes other worthy testimonies that add positive proof that Jesus Christ is the Source of real and lasting change. He captures in order to set His captives free. This powerful story of God's mercy will hopefully lead others to the Chain Breaker, Jesus Christ.

Don Wilkerson

President, Brooklyn Teen Challenge

INTRODUCTION

Hopeless. One word could describe the condition of my life as I sat on the edge of my bed in my tenth and final treatment center. Death seemed to be the best and only solution for the mess I'd made and the life I'd destroyed. There had always been a light at the end of the tunnel – some glimmer of hope that a better day would come. Until now. I'd prayed many times in my life, but never this prayer: "Lord, I give up. Just take my life. Please, I don't want to live anymore."

It wasn't the first time I'd lost everything in my addiction. I'd become accustomed to, and quite frankly very skilled at, picking up the scattered pieces of my broken life. When I was 20 I moved from my hometown in Minnesota to Florida to try to escape my druggie friends and lifestyle. I thought getting enough miles between us would solve all my problems. For a while, it did. But the problem wasn't them. It was me. Something inside of me – a dangerous, evil, unquenchable thirst for the thrills of drugs and alcohol – a monster so strong and so powerful I thought killing myself was the only way to get rid of it for good. Chaos and crisis were a regular part of my existence. I can't even keep track of all the times I tried to move away for a fresh start. From Minnesota to Denver, back to Minnesota, to Florida, back to Minnesota again, then New York, California, and eventually back to Minnesota. I was the queen of one-way tickets.

After losing a job, I'd find another. Burned bridges with friends and shattered relationships didn't me. I'd move to a new city and make new friends. Credibility, reputation, trust, position, and accomplishments all went out the window. But I knew that trust could always be regained with consistent good behavior over time. If you make a big enough mess and hurt enough people, you have two options. Fight or flight. You can run away and try to forget about the people and the mess, or you can do the hard thing and fight to rebuild all that was lost. I was a runner. I would run away and get sober. I was an expert at getting sober. It was staying sober that I just couldn't quite seem to figure out.

Loss was a way of life to me, my one constant friend. Loss of trust, loss of progress, loss of friends, loss of family – I was no stranger to these things. I lost everything so many times in my addiction, but my one saving grace was that each time I'd gained it back. Maddening as the cycle was, chaos and crisis always preceded restoration and hope. This became my normal. No matter how big the mess, in time I'd pick up the pieces of my broken life. Chaos was inevitable, but I always had believed that I could bounce back. But this time was different. This was the first time in the midst of losing everything that I actually lost my hope.

Hope is a powerful thing. It's one of those things that you will never quite appreciate until it's gone. Desperately addicted to meth, I no longer believed there was a chance that my life could get any better. I was fully convinced that the people in my life would be better off without me. Meth had completely consumed my life. Meth decided when and if I slept or ate. Meth decided where I spent my time and money. It had me. All of me. In between ambulance trips and emergency room visits I stayed in cheap hotels getting high alone. Wasting away, I was a strung-out junkie running out of time and money. I was convinced that my purpose in life was to die alone with a needle in my arm so that I could be an example to others of what not to do.

Some people say it's darkest just before the dawn. I'm writing my story because I have seen a shade of darkness that pen and ink cannot describe. But I have seen a light that shines even brighter – so bright that the darkness cannot help but flee.

I am writing for the drug addict sitting in a dirty basement with a needle in her arm. I am writing for the perfectionist who is so empty inside she tries to cover it up by being the best. I'm writing for the innocent child who was abused and neglected. I'm writing for the athlete who has to win because his worth depends on it. I am writing for the good person who is only good because he needs people to applaud him. I am writing for every person who has ever resolved to try harder and do better. I am writing for every lost soul, every wandering prodigal, every prisoner and anyone who has ever lost it all.

I'm passionate about telling people the truth about who God is and what He can do. I have several friends who have equally powerful stories of tragedy, hardship, and overcoming adversity through Jesus. You'll meet them at the end of my book. Each friend has included their email or other ways to get in touch, so if you are moved by their stories, please reach out to them.

Also, throughout my years in darkness I kept many journals. I wrote when I was drunk and high and lost and also while I was getting sober in treatment. They are full of first hand accounts of my life story, my emotions, and my struggles. Throughout this book you will find *real* journal entries from some of the darkest and most devastating days of my life. I hope that you are touched by these stories.

Lastly, this book holds nothing back. I share extremely personal information and so do the other storytellers – things like abuse and suicide, self-harm, depression, and other mature content. There are very real and raw moments of despair so I caution young people reading this to ask your parents to read it first to make sure they are comfortable with you reading it.

Jesus was and is the light that called me out of darkness. And in the greatest book ever written, He calls those of us who belong to Him more than conquerors.

One of my heroes in Christianity is Christine Caine. She is a speaker, author, and activist who has devoted her life to helping people find Jesus. I once heard Christine say that to be more than a conqueror means that not only have we overcome our past, but that God is now using our past to give *someone else* a future.

Thank you for picking up my book. Thank you for reading my story. It is because of you that I am more than a conqueror. I pray that my story and the stories of my friends inspire you to have hope and a future. Please know that no matter what you are facing, you can be overwhelmingly victorious through Christ. Nothing is impossible for Him!

THE EARLY DAYS

I'm a dreamer. I've always been a dreamer. When I was a kid I dreamed of growing up and being a famous singer, an office manager, a paleontologist, an actress, an English teacher. I dreamed of being a lawyer and a chef and an artist. I never dreamed of growing up and becoming a drug addict or a college dropout. I never thought I'd be homeless, in and out of drug treatment centers and in psych wards. That type of thing was unthinkable for me. I was a good kid.

I grew up in a house in the suburbs with my mom and dad. I had two older sisters - who are eight and nine years older than me - a dog, and a pool. Life was pretty good. Sure, my family was far from perfect. My parents had their marital issues like any husband and wife do. I remember my parents breaking up a lot. One day we'd be a normal family, and the next day my dad would be moving out. Eventually he would move back in and they would try to work it out. As a child with limited understanding of emotion and the human psyche, trying to process all of this on my own was very troubling. I didn't realize until years later how much I blamed myself for not being "lovable" enough for them to want to stay together. I couldn't understand at the time why they didn't love each other. Part of me wanted to be the hero and save the day by being so extraordinary that they couldn't help but stay in love. As the baby of the family I thought there must have been something I could do to keep them together.

Aside from that, I was bright and imaginative. Others may have called me bossy, but I prefer to think I was a natural born leader. I would hang out with the neighborhood kids, inventing games and making up the rules as we went along. I was an entrepreneur, creating income by painting rocks and trying to sell them and other crazy ideas that my brain manufactured. I had ideas - good ones- well ok not all of them were good – but I believed in them so much I could convince anyone they needed a neon pink painted rock.

Not only was I the leader of the pack around the neighborhood, I was an <u>excellent</u> student. School was easy for me and I <u>excelled</u> (excellent- then excelled- maybe find a different word for variation) at it. I had plenty of friends in elementary school, straight A's, and I was always the teacher's pet. I listened and applied myself. I was a likable kid. I stayed out of trouble and if at all possible, I went above and beyond what was required of me.

In addition to a vibrant social and educational life, I was a gifted athlete and performer. After a brief stint with dance and gymnastics, I found my calling on the ice rink. I started figure skating and quickly advanced up the ranks in my classes. I began taking private lessons. I loved skating. When I stepped onto the ice the sense of freedom and grace I felt was like no other. Competitions and ice shows provided the opportunity to have all eyes on me, and I loved knowing the fact that I was the girl to watch, and the one to try to beat. First place trophies piled up on the shelves in my bedroom and I was never satisfied with second place.

The feelings of being different started in those locker rooms. The majority of the skaters in my club were pretty white girls. I was one of the only minorities. I often looked at their blonde hair and blue eyes with envy. I don't think it was the color of my skin that bothered me, but the fact that I was different. I stood out in team photos. My body type was more muscular. My hair was curly. I just wanted to be like everybody else. Perhaps I had no grounds upon which to base my identity and worth besides my appearance and performance. Perhaps I thought if I could look the best and be the best, I'd be worth something to someone. Perhaps I thought I'd be worth enough to my parents to look past their differences and stick out their marriage in true love. Perhaps.

So there began the striving in my life. Ice rinks, classrooms, recess, at home–I was constantly striving. On the outside I had everything going for me. People like me didn't end up addicted to drugs. People like me were not those you'd see on anti-meth billboards with scabs on their faces, missing teeth, and thinning hair from their drug abuse. People like me ended up at the top of their class in Ivy League colleges, on Olympic platforms, and naturally successful. At the very least people like me ended up succeeding in college, getting a fulfilling job, getting married, having 2 kids, a dog, and a white picket fence. So what happened? Where did things go wrong?

TURNING POINT

During my sixth grade school year my self-consciousness spread like wildfire from the locker room to the classroom. The feeling of being different plagued me daily, making me feel uncomfortable in my own skin. I wanted a place to fit in, convinced that if I could just find it, that feeling would go away. No matter where I went or what I did, I always felt like I did not belong. Other people seemed to be so confident in who they were, or just so completely oblivious that it didn't matter to them if they seemed to fit in or not. I wondered if the dialogue in my head was obvious to other people around me.

Sixth grade would be my last year in elementary school and I'd be off to junior high the following year. I remember looking at my friend group in elementary school and thinking we were kind of dorky. We were the smart, quiet kids. We didn't have cool clothes. We had friends because we were nice, not because we were popular. I made a decision that the summer after sixth grade would be the summer that I'd reinvent myself. When I started at my new school in junior high as a seventh grader I was going to be cool. I was going to ditch my friends and do whatever I needed to do to be popular.

That summer I went to a trendy clothing store and bought en entire wardrobe worth of clothes that I thought would be really cool and fashion-forward. The movie, "Clueless," came out and I modeled my fashion after the so-called most popular girls in Beverly Hills. Many of you reading this are way too young to remember this movie but you can Google it! I watched the movie over and over, even trying to learn some of the language they used. I brought everything I learned into seventh grade with my best friend by my side. We were the self-proclaimed Cher and Dionne of Brooklyn Junior High.

There was one problem. Our school was in the suburbs of Minneapolis, a far cry from Beverly Hills. My strategy completely backfired. Not only were we unpopular, we stuck out like a couple of sore thumbs. The popular kids at Brooklyn Junior were more sporty than trendy. My best friend traded her mini skirt and high heels for a basketball jersey and sneakers. I loved my new style, however, and wasn't ready to let it go. It felt like I finally found who I was and my clothes were an expression of my creativity and individuality. I quickly became the butt of many jokes and even started receiving threats. People hated me because I was different. Some girls even followed me around school making fun of me, calling me a "valley girl," and threatening to beat me up.

I was trying so hard to find friends and fit in, but it didn't work. I was alone to navigate a new school. I tried to survive by getting involved with music and sports. I joined the school choir and discovered my love for music. I joined the swim team and found the rush of competition in another sport very enjoyable. I ignored the loneliness inside and unbeknownst to me at the time, found my worth in achievement and performance. I tried to ignore the taunting threats from the bullies, but they intensified every day until I couldn't take it anymore.

They didn't take bullying as seriously in school

back then as they do now. I remember coming home crying every day, dreading going to school. I desperately wanted people to like me. I couldn't understand why people didn't like me, and I began to not even like myself.

I went to the principal's office and complained about the bullying. Sadly, I was not met with any compassion or support. The principal's response was that I was just having "social issues" and because the girls hadn't physically laid a hand on me, I was just going to have to "figure it out". He said there was nothing he could do. Disappointed, confused, and scared, I walked out of his office unsure of how to face another day at my school.

I was twelve years old. I had one friend – my best friend – who ditched me and joined forces with the very group of girls who were making fun of me. Left alone, all I wanted was to be liked. To go deeper, all I really wanted was to be loved. To be fully known, and fully loved. In my little twelve-year-old mind I decided that I was not lovable. My parents must not love me, because if they did, they'd stay together. Kids at school didn't love me – they hated me – that wasn't hard to figure out. There really wasn't a safe place for me to go. I desperately wanted to run into the arms of someone who could love me and protect me. Someone who could understand my pain, and tell me they were so sorry I had to go through it all, and that I wasn't alone. I wanted someone to tell me that everything was going to be okay. But for me, there were no such arms to embrace. I didn't have a safe place. I didn't know there was a God who cared about me. I just thought I was all alone.

My parents saw the pain was beginning to take its toll on me. We lived in a school district that did not have open enrollment for junior high, which meant that if you lived in a certain school zone, you were required to attend that school. You did not have the option to attend another school and commute until high school.

My parents stepped in and actually sold the house that we lived in, and bought a house on the other side of town so that I could go to a different school. My best friend's parents had actually gotten divorced and she had to move. Even though I was upset about how she ditched me at Brooklyn Junior, I forgave her and we remained friends. She'd been going to this new school and told me about how different and great it was. I couldn't wait to start at my new school. It was way more diverse, and I already had an "in" with the cool kids since my friend was part of that clique.

I had high hopes going into my first day at the new school, and I knew it was going to be the perfect fresh start that I needed.

A NEW BEGINNING

Life at my new school was even better than I could've imagined. With no effort of my own, I was instantly accepted into the popular crowd. My three best friends were (the prettiest girls in school with the coolest clothes and the most exciting social lives)-use language that jumps out more "were stunning, dressed like movie stars and had social lives like them too". Being at the dead center of popularity felt amazing. It was like a dream come true; I had finally "arrived". We were in eighth grade, but we were the only group that got invited to all the ninth grade parties. And these weren't just any ninth graders. They too were the cool, attractive, sought after social crew.

A lot of the guys were already playing on some

of the high school sports teams so we'd also get invited to high school football and hockey games. I couldn't believe it was my life. I had so many friends and I was having so much fun.

But I still remembered. Underneath the surface of my smiles and joy lingered deep feelings of insecurity and rejection. I never took the time to process or heal from what happened at Brooklyn Junior because my feelings got blurred in the excitement of my newfound acceptance. Everything that happened to me – getting laughed at, made fun of, having no friends and more enemies than a twelve year old knows what to do with – it impacted me down to the core. I was so scared of getting to that place again where everyone hated me. I even hated myself at times. I often thought there had to be something so wrong with me for so many people to hate me so much.

Then one night I got invited to a house of one of the popular girls. A bunch of the girls were hanging out there and someone's older sister had purchased a bottle of hard liquor. I didn't know when my mom was giving me a ride to have a sleepover with my new friends that this is what they were doing. I hadn't really given much thought to alcohol. I'd never made a decision as to whether or not I'd try it and I didn't have much of an opinion of it being good or bad. My parents drank alcohol and I knew both of my older sisters had tried it. So when the opportunity presented itself to drink I didn't think twice.

People always throw around the term "Peer Pressure." It sounds so clinical. So black and white. I didn't feel pressured by my friends into drinking that night. They never said they'd ditch me if I didn't drink with them. But I desperately wanted to keep them as my friends. I figured I better just do what they were doing and not make it awkward or draw any attention to myself. Insecurity had already crept back in and I wondered if I was pretty enough and cool enough to be friends with these girls. They were way prettier than the face I saw in the mirror. The voice in my head was constantly telling me I didn't belong and it was only a matter of time until they'd realize I wasn't worthy of them and reject me. The fear of rejection grew more intense as time went on.

Determined to make it seem like I'd drank a dozen times before, I took one shot. Then another. And another. Much to my surprise, alcohol had an effect on me that night I couldn't believe. It was so fun. It took away the voice inside wondering if people really liked me. It even made me like myself more. I looked in the mirror and saw a beautiful, confident girl who was worthy of friends and attention. Alcohol helped me out of the shell that I'd crawled into for protection from the bullies. When I drank I could strike up a conversation with anyone. I could tell jokes and stories and make people laugh and I felt like a better version of myself.

We drank many times after my first encounter without anything bad ever happening. We didn't get caught. There was no drama or trouble. Besides throwing up a time or two, there were no other consequences. This caused me to begin to believe the lie that alcohol was completely harmless. I loved how it made me feel. Every time I had a chance to drink I did. We'd drink on the weekends, before school dances, before and during football games. We'd sneak clear alcohol in our water bottles. We definitely drank to get a buzz, and we usually ended up pretty wasted. At least I did.

Alcohol seemed like the solution to every problem I could think of and I fell in love with the way it made me feel. Once in awhile I'd drink too much, throw up and feel really miserable, but it happened to my friends too so I didn't think too much of it. I was having so much fun bonding with my new friends over all of our drinking adventures. Each party solidified my position with the popular crowd. All I wanted was to press pause and hold onto those moments forever.

THE TIME OF MY LIFE

In health classes they talk to you about substance abuse prevention. They tell you that alcohol is a gateway drug. I believe that with all my heart. I often wonder where my life would be if I'd waited until I was legally old enough to drink. What if I never took a drink at all? Alcohol opened the door for my curiosity to try other drugs. In eighth grade, drugs like cocaine and meth sounded super scary to me. I told myself I'd never touch hardcore drugs like that. But marijuana didn't sound so bad.

Drinking alcohol started to become boring and predictable. I got used to the feeling of the buzz and of being drunk. I saw other people at parties smoking marijuana and I was curious. I knew it was illegal, but the people smoking it were people I looked up to. They were popular, older, cool kids. If they were doing it, I figured it couldn't be that bad.

I knew I wasn't going to seek it out, but if someone offered it to me I'd definitely try it. One Friday night I had my chance. I was at a high school party with a few of my friends. One of my girl-friends had an older sister in high school and she threw the party because their parents were out of town. I felt so cool because we were the only junior high kids invited. We started drinking early that night. We passed bottles of different kinds of hard liquor, took giant drinks from the bottle, grabbed a soda to chase it, and passed it to the next person, laughing and cringing because it was so disgusting. Soon after we started drinking I had a decent buzz going from drinking alcohol. I saw some kids in a room upstairs with the door closed and I knew that they were smoking weed. I decided to go in and pretend like I was looking for a bathroom or some-thing – any excuse to get closer to the drugs. I figured they would probably offer it to me, and they did.

Smoking weed was not a good feeling to add to my alcohol buzz. Dizzy, anxious, and nauseous, I regretted smoking it. I wondered why people touched the stuff! Still somehow I got the idea that I needed to try it again when I hadn't been drinking to see if it was any different. The next time I tried smoking weed was after school with some of my friends. We hadn't been drinking. This time I began to understand why people smoke the stuff. I laughed until my stomach hurt, binged out on junk food, laughed some more, and then passed out to take a nap. I am not saying this to try to glorify the drugs. Alcohol and marijuana opened the door for me to try other drugs, which completely took a hold of my life. No one wakes up one day and says, "I think I'll be a drug addict, stick needles in my arm, and go to rehab ten times." I'm saying this because there's a reason people do this, and it *is* fun at first. But then it's a gradual descent. You take one step in the wrong direction, and before you know it you're rationalizing and doing things you never thought you would. What previously seemed evil now just looks sort of bad. You take another step, and another, and another, and now what once seemed unthinkable appears to be almost harmless. I never would have tried harder drugs if I hadn't already been smoking and drinking. But that's not how you think when you're doing it in the moment. You're only thinking about how good it feels and how fun it is. That's the allure of it. It was a trap. The temporary high was nothing compared to how low things would soon become.

The high from smoking weed was a lot different than the buzz from alcohol. Weed made my mind kind of foggy and I could just zone out and laugh. I liked that smoking weed didn't make me feel sick or give me a next day hangover.

I was still fairly active in sports, but the one thing that was really tough to do was figure skating. Smoking weed made it harder for me to breathe. I could still do other activities if I was high, like volleyball and school, but figure skating really killed my buzz.

One decision I made because of my addiction changed the course of my life forever. I still think about it to this day and wonder what my life would have been like if I hadn't made that decision. Most days after school I went to figure skating practice. Once upon a time, it was the thing I day-dreamed about all day at school. I couldn't wait until the final bell rang and I could head over to the arena. All I wanted to do was get my skates laced up and smell the ice. The sound of blades crunching the ice beneath my feet brought a smile to my face and the thought of getting on the ice was the only thing that got me through history and math class some days!

But this day I didn't want to go to practice because I wanted to get high. I knew I couldn't do both. A temporary high won the battle that day, over years of practice, dedication, excellence, and the thing I truly enjoyed the most in life. I decided I wanted to get high that day and I did not go to skating practice. In fact, I never went to practice again. I quit figure skating that day. It was the end of a lifelong dream. I've often regretted that decision. I wish I had a mentor at the time, or someone in my life who could've talked me through my decision of quitting and uncovered the drug use. I wish someone could've explained to me the potential outcome of walking the path I was beginning to go down.

I couldn't see it at the time, but this was the beginning of alcohol and drugs taking over my life. They were changing my personality, my interests, and my goals. They were commandeering my habits, my hobbies, and my heart. But I couldn't see it. I thought I was having the time of my life.

I started high school with excitement because I knew there would be better parties, more weekend excuses to drink and get high. I was still part of the popular crowd, but high school was much different. Within the popular crowd there were different cliques. There were the jocks who didn't drink because sports were so important to them. There were the jocks who drank a ton and knew about all the college parties. There were the pretty, studious, social butterfly girls. There were the party kids. There were the popular athletic girls who played varsity basketball and volleyball.

In all the little sub-divisions of cool kids, I began to be drawn more to the party crowd. I'd dropped out of skating and wasn't good enough at any other sport to make varsity. I was still a straight-A student, but school was always something that came very naturally to me. I was a bright kid and didn't have to try too hard to get perfect grades. But I wasn't interested in going out for student council or any leadership role, and I wasn't engaged in any way. I just wanted to party. School was something I did in between parties, because I was required to. School was a place for crushes on older guys and sitting at the popular table at lunch.

The drinking got worse in high school. Most of the time I drank I got really wasted and made a fool of myself so I started to get a reputation of being a lush. In my sophomore year of high school, a few rumors were spread about me and I could tell people were gossiping about me when I'd walk in a room or sit at a table. I had a secret that I'd confided in one of my best friends but she turned on me and told everyone. I was devastated. It felt like in one day I went from having two hundred friends to having two hundred enemies. It was like junior high all over again but a hundred times worse. I couldn't even walk to my locker without getting dirty looks and being called horrible names right to my face.

Socially exiled, I moved my locker away from the popular kids back to a section of lockers in a hallway that my friends and I used to call, "dirtball hall." This was where a lot of the hardcore party kids hung out. These kids came to school on acid and mushrooms, dealt drugs, went to raves, and they always looked high on something. I'm pretty sure they were the only kids in school who hadn't heard the rumors about me. Or if they had heard, they were probably too high to care. They became my people. I became a part of their tribe.

Not long after I started hanging out with them I began experimenting with harder drugs. By the time I was 15, I'd tried tripping on acid and mushrooms and was quickly on my way to becoming a drug addict. I started to talk differently, dress differently, laugh less and care less about what people thought of me. High school years went on and I'd started going to underground rave parties and getting high on ecstasy. I'd get such a rush of happiness and euphoria on ecstasy, I couldn't believe it was possible to feel that way. But the next day, I'd sink into such a low depression I wouldn't want to get out of bed unless there was a chemical involved to make me feel better. Eventually I'd built up a tolerance to ecstasy and I couldn't really feel anything by taking just one pill. I'd heard a lot of stories about people who died from taking it. Because of that I made the decision to stick to one pill. Eventually I just stopped wasting my money when one pill wasn't doing anything for me. I'd get so jealous of people I'd take with me to parties because we'd take the same pill and I'd see them feeling so incredible because it was only their first or second time.

It was around that time that someone introduced me to cocaine. I'd never snorted any drug up my nose. The first time I did it, it burned like crazy but it gave me a better feeling than any high I'd ever had. It wasn't like alcohol or weed or any psychedelic drugs because I was clear minded. I could walk fine, talk fine, drive fine. It just made me feel really clear headed, really decisive, and really alive. I had rushes of ideas. Creativity was something I'd lost in my addiction but when I was high on cocaine, it stimulated the creative part of my brain and I suddenly wanted to draw, to paint, to write stories and poetry again. I also loved cocaine because it solved my problem of drinking too much. When it came to alcohol, enough was never enough. I always wanted one more drink.. I'd often black out or find myself vomiting in some bathroom; yet I'd still want more. Cocaine allowed me to drink more alcohol, so it was a win-win situation from my perspective.

I was still having the time of my life. Being a druggie was Plan B for me, because I didn't succeed at being popular. But I embraced it and as long as I was high. I was loving life. I never got caught, I didn't get in trouble, I was still on the A-honor roll. I was a star student. My clothes and physical appearance had changed but I'm sure from the outside looking in I seemed like your average adolescent struggling through teenage-angst, hormonal changes, and whatever phase I was in..

At home, I was a moody teenager. Depression crept in and I started seeing doctors and therapists to feel better. I told them all my symptoms but I never told them I was on drugs, so they put me on antidepressants. I didn't tell them I had taken a ton of ecstasy, and I certainly wasn't educated about the effects of drugs on the brain. All I knew was that if I wasn't going to get drunk or high I didn't really want to get out of bed. I was always sad and had a melancholic outlook on the future. I missed my old life, having fun with my friends, and I spent a lot of time drinking alone in my room and stealing alcohol from my parent's liquor cabinet. I started drinking alone and smoking weed everyday before school. Somehow I always kept good grades, which convinced me that all the stuff the teachers tell you in health class about drugs being bad was either lies or scare tactics.

After all the social drama in my sophomore year, things calmed down a bit my junior year. By senior year, so many other dramatic things had happened that many of my old friends took me back. But it wasn't the same. I'd missed out on so much time with them, and I didn't know if they were really my friends or not. I didn't trust that they wouldn't shut me out again, so I didn't try to get attached. Alcohol and drugs were my new best friends. No matter what party I went to, or which group of friends I was with, I got as drunk or as high as I could on whatever anybody had to offer me. I was comfortably numb. I never dealt with any of it. I just drank or snorted my problems away.

On graduation day I was drunk and high walking the platform in my cap and gown, graduating with honors. My motto in life was "druggies can succeed!" No one could convince me otherwise because I was living proof. But my "success" didn't last much longer.

THE DARK SIDE

The summer after I graduated high school opened the door to the darkest days I'd ever experienced in my life. I'd started to develop an increased tolerance to cocaine. While I loved the rush of the high, I was beginning to need more and more to feel it. Cocaine was expensive, and I didn't have a job at the time. The little bit of money I'd get from my parents each week wasn't enough to support my habit. Thankfully, a lot of my friends were generous with what they had. We'd all hang out and share our drugs and alcohol and we didn't really keep track of who had what. We just shared with each other to keep the party going.

I remember one night I had a bizarre dream. I was at a friend's house, enjoying myself, and someone came around with this huge pillowcase full of white crystals. They were sparkling and had an allure of magic and power to them. I wanted those crystals more than anything in the dream. I woke up and didn't think much of it. Interestingly enough, the next day I was hanging with a friend I'd always done cocaine with. He pulled out a mirror with a line of white powder, but it looked different than cocaine. He offered it to me and told me it was meth. I was so scared to try it. I'd heard of crystal meth before and everyone I knew of who was into meth was really odd. I know they'd stay awake for days on end without eating or sleeping. They'd commit crimes and carry guns. They'd steal from people and were missing teeth. They were really sketchy people, constantly paranoid and almost delusional.

But my friend assured me that if I liked cocaine, meth was just like it, only better and cheaper. That was a selling point for me because cocaine was getting expensive. I had to snort a line about every 15 minutes to stay up.

I tried meth that day and it was as if the heavens opened up and I'd found the wonder drug. I did one tiny line and I was high for several hours. I felt more alive than I could remember ever feeling before. As soon as I came down, I wanted more.

Trying meth was one of the most consequential decisions of my entire life. I had no idea it would ever lead me to homelessness, psych wards, hospitals, courtrooms, emptiness, depression, and thoughts consumed by suicide and death.

Over the course of the next two years, my life changed dramatically. I dropped out of college three times, dated a meth dealer (who later died of an overdose), and lived a life that revolved around meth. My boyfriend and I would stay up for weeks at a time using meth. We sold drugs to sketchy people and I saw people who were so addicted and desperate, they'd do anything to get high. If they didn't have money they'd try to give us things like cars, electronics, and guns for trade.

My boyfriend had been using meth for much longer than me and he'd actually switched to needles to get high. I'd watch him do a smaller amount than I was doing, but get really, really high and I started to get jealous. It seemed like a different rush than just snorting and I wanted to try it. For a long time he refused to teach me how to do it. He said needles had ruined his life and turned him into a slave and he didn't want to see that happen to me or have anything to do with contributing to it. I was relentless in asking and eventually he gave in. I will forever remember the first time I used a needle to get high.

I was instantly hooked and never wanted to go back to snorting. I too became a slave. Meth became the reason I faced each day. Meth decided where I went and what I did. Meth decided who my friends were. I remember not wanting to go to family gatherings unless I was high. Not long after I first tried meth I became physically dependent on it. Without meth I couldn't stay awake. Then when I'd get high, the last place I wanted to be was around family. I didn't want people asking me why I was so skinny or why I wasn't eating or what I was up to these days. I'd dropped out of college, I wasn't able to keep a job, and I didn't have any real friends. Really, all I did was meth.

Meanwhile, my older sisters had gotten married and started families. Their kids were growing up and they were so precious and innocent. I remember thinking I should stay far away from them because they were so young and impressionable. I felt that I had become such a dangerous and evil person and didn't want the little kids to be around someone who was such a bad influence. I didn't want them thinking I was great or, even worse, trying to become anything like me.

As I progressed in my addiction, things got worse. I was swallowed up in a life of darkness. I saw friends getting sent to jail, prison, and going to treatment. I heard of people overdosing, and several people I knew even died. I started to look around me and see what was becoming of people and I began to wonder what would become of me.

I remember having a concept of God. I believed He was real, and I also believed the devil was real. Quite frankly, I thought I looked the devil right in the eyes of some of the people I'd met. I clung to the darkness. It was my safe place. I always knew there was light in me, but I didn't know how to live without meth.

I'd often have spiritual conversations with people, debating the existence of God. I always argued there was a God, but he wanted nothing to do with people like me. People like me belonged to the devil. People would always tell me I was different, nice, pure, or good, and that I didn't belong in the slums of drug life. I kind of felt that way too and I could spot others who were different or nice or didn't belong. It was like we still had our souls. Addicts can seem like dark, corrupted, soul-less shells of humans – empty people walking around with no conscience or regard for morality. But I always felt like I still had my soul. I was just in a dark season of life and I would get out eventually. I believed I'd quit eventually. I just wasn't ready to give up the meth life quite yet.

Maybe that was because I had a family member share the Gospel with me sometime in my early teens. I don't remember much of the conversation, except that he told me that the world was possibly going to end, or I would die, and when either of these events happened I would either spend eternity in heaven with Jesus or in hell. I cried and said a frightened "repeat after me" prayer and I guess that was when I handed my eternal life over to Jesus. But after that prayer, I never really read a Bible or prayed much or went to church after that. Nothing changed for me after that conversation. I still believed in heaven and hell. But life on meth was a dark prison. I honestly felt that if I died and went to hell it would be a step up from the life I was living. Chained to the god of meth, I was stuck in a death-grip, with no exit in sight.

I do believe God took that decision very seriously, even if I did not. Through all the meth and evil and darkness, there was a deep and nagging sense within me that my life could change, that things could get better. I just didn't know when or how.

Using meth was a vicious cycle, and while it felt good at the beginning, I started to feel like I was trapped. I wanted out. I began to try to quit using. My boyfriend and I would both commit to getting sober. The physical withdrawal from meth is unbelievably difficult. You constantly eat and sleep for days at a time. You feel absolutely depressed. You know just a little meth will save you. We couldn't stay strong. One of us would be strong, the other would cave in, and soon enough we'd be jumping in the car, heading to pick up at our drug dealer's place. It was a vicious cycle. I would have terrible nightmares when I was in withdrawal. I dreamed of hell and demons and using meth. I'd wake up in cold sweats, scared to fall back asleep, knowing the only way I could stay awake and avoid the nightmares was to get high.

After many failed attempts at getting sober, and relapses, and disappointment, I realized that if I was going to get sober I wasn't going to be able to do it in Minnesota. I knew way too many drug dealers. A friend of the family lived in Florida and had an extra room because her daughter who was my age was off in college. She agreed to let me stay with her to try to get back on my feet. A lot of people believed in me and wanted to see me get away from the influence of my drug dealer boyfriend. So I left, intending to leave my old life behind, and never see my boyfriend or drug addict friends again.

I bought a one-way ticket and was off to the sunshine state for a fresh start. The idea of a new beginning once again sounded refreshing and I was desperately ready for change. It was really tough to go through the withdrawals, but I was in a place where I could sleep and eat as much as I needed to, and there was absolutely zero access to meth. I made it through. Unfortunately, I rediscovered my passion for alcohol to help me through the meth withdrawal process. I started drinking more heavily than ever before. I blacked out almost every time I drank, and I started making really stupid decisions. One night I completely shaved my head and got behind the wheel of a car after drinking too much vodka. Apparently I thought I would drive all the way back to Minnesota, but instead I crashed the car and stumbled away, bald on the streets of Florida in the middle of the night. The police picked me up and didn't know what to do with me, so they threw me in the psych ward. I had a lot of explaining to do when the alcohol wore off. I managed to escape the situation without getting into any real trouble. I don't remember what I said as the alcohol wore off, but I remember thinking I'd gotten really lucky and I vowed to never get behind the wheel again after I'd been drinking. That was one of many promises I made to myself and others that would eventually be broken.

Deciding to move on with the process of rebuilding my life, I found a job waiting tables at a restaurant near my place. I thought my drinking might slow down as soon as I had the responsibility of a full time job. I began to make friends at the restaurant. A few of my friends were musicians who often played at a bar downtown. They'd invite me to come but I was only 20. They said I shouldn't worry. Because I was with them, I could get in without showing an ID. And if anyone asked, they'd just vouch for me and say I was 21. I enjoyed the bar scene, having friends that were fun and social, and really liked my new life in Florida.

I didn't share with anyone why I moved there. No one knew about my past or what I was running from. They just knew me as the new girl who was cool and wanted to get to know me.

There were two coworkers at the restaurant that

were really intriguing to me. One of the guys I observed from afar. He was quiet, he never seemed to get upset or frazzled when things got super busy, and he always seemed available to lend a hand to people when they needed it. He didn't swear like everyone else did, he didn't go out for smoke breaks, and I never saw him at the bars or parties after work. I wondered what was so different about him, but never really got to know him.

There was another guy with a similar character, minus the drinking. He was blonde haired, blue eyed, had a loud and electric personality, a huge grin from ear to ear, and always helped out with things. He eventually became one of my closest friends in Florida. I decided it was time to move out of the place I was living, and since I was working and had friends I wanted to be independent. He happened to need a roommate, so I moved in. We got along really well. We had tons of mutual friends. He was dating a girl and I just adored her, things were starting to look up and I was starting to enjoy life again.

My roommate was different. He went to Christian college. He told me he'd gone on mission trips. I'd never heard of such a thing. He told me stories about how he spent hours in a rickety truck driving uphill to some village on top of a mountain to bring food and Bibles to kids. He talked about sharing the gospel with them and I wasn't even really sure what that meant. It struck me as so odd that someone so young would actually pay money to go help people. I didn't know anybody like that.

The years I spent in Florida were both devastating and beautiful. It was in Florida that God began to reveal himself to me. Maybe God had been trying for a really long time. But Florida was where I started to notice. Somewhere along the way someone invited me to a church service. I don't know why I accepted the invitation, but I went. I hadn't been to church in years. But something in me felt lost. I didn't know where to go to get found again, but I knew it wasn't bars or the liquor store. I took the invitation and visited the church. Walking through those doors I had no idea what to expect. Completely alone and out of my element, it was a bold move.

The church experience was way different than I'd expected. I was surprised to see people playing guitars. These were young people like me. They looked cool. They looked happy. I watched them walk around and it seemed as though they walked with purpose. They had something I didn't. It was more than the pep in their step and the twinkle in their eye. I didn't know it at the time, but they had Jesus.

I didn't know what was different about the church people. But I liked being around them. I'd never been to a church that was young and fun. I'd been to my grandparents' church a few times growing up. I was the only little black kid in the room. They sang hymns and had grey hair and all I remember was how I felt when everyone said the Lord's prayer and the words weren't printed in the bulletin. I flipped through the pages frantically, studying the front and back of each page twice. I desperately wanted to find the words before it was over and as soon as I realized they were all saying it from memory, I was convinced of one thing: I don't belong here. From that day forward I wasn't too interested in church, although the cookies after service were something to look forward to.

Things took a turn for the worse for me after I visited that church in Florida. I was still going out for drinks after work with my friends. Often times I'd find myself drinking alone in my room, drinking in the morning before work, and many times I got behind the wheel, despite what I'd promised myself. But I kept going to church on Sundays. I thought maybe if I spent enough time around those people, it'd rub off and eventually I'd become like them. The drinking began to take over my life. I wondered if I was an alcoholic because when I started drinking, I couldn't stop. But I didn't drink every day, so I wasn't sure. I thought alcoholics needed to drink every day and that definitely wasn't me. I was an avid runner. I kept a steady job, and I was functional in all other aspects of my life. I'd never gotten into any legal trouble or had serious consequences from drinking, besides obviously my shaved head and the wrecked car. But then one night I got behind the wheel after binge drinking myself in a blackout. I ended up crashing the vehicle into a pole and woke up in jail with my first legal charge. I was charged with a DUI (Driving Under the Influence). I couldn't believe it had happened to me. I'd never been to court. It sounded so scary. I had to get dressed up, appear in front of a judge, and plead guilty to the charges. My dad flew down from Minnesota to get me out of jail. I was embarrassed and scared, and I wished I could have turned back time and never gotten behind the wheel that night.

As punishment for my crime, my license was suspended and I was put on probation. I had to attend AA meetings and alcohol education classes. I bummed rides from my friends to work. And on Sundays, I rode my bike to church. I was just doing what I had to do to get my license reinstated, but in my heart I wasn't ready to stop drinking. I saw this as a wakeup call to be more careful. I could drink. I just couldn't drink and drive.

I was a hard worker at my jobs and I had the reputation of a goody two shoes. I didn't really swear. I tried to be kind to people. There were a few kitchen staff that other servers would pick on or be mean to, but I always felt for the underdog so I made a point to talk to them and be nice.

I started to feel torn between the emptiness of my life, which consisted of basically working and drinking, and a better life that I wondered whether or not existed for me. I often reflected on my life and my heart was searching for meaning. I thought there had to be more to life than how I was living. There had to be a reason why I was alive. I just couldn't find it. Then, one night, things came to a crashing halt in Florida. I was at a party with my coworkers. We were all drinking, which was nothing out of the ordinary. I noticed a few people seemed kind of different than their usual drinking selves, but I didn't think much of it. I'd seen one of my coworkers walk into a side room earlier, and when the conversation fell flat in the kitchen I decided to relocate. I walked into that side room and it was as if time stood still. It was just like a scene in the movies where everything is loud and spinning and suddenly the music stops and you could hear a pin drop. All eyes were on me.

They were snorting lines of cocaine and in walks miss goody two shoes. I'm sure they all thought they were busted or that they should hide it from me because I was so sweet and innocent. I should have walked away. I stood there, baffled, with a decision to make. If I could go back to my 22 year-old self in that moment, I would have screamed, "Run! Flee! Your life depends on it!" But 22 year old me gave in to impulse and that old familiar feeling. For a moment time stood still, until I broke the silence with a life-altering response: "I'll take some!" No one in the room would have predicted my response would be to ask for a line of cocaine. They passed the next line to me.

I'd forgotten how it felt, but it all came quickly rushing back to me. The high, the rush, the endorphins, and eventually the shame and regret. Nothing had changed. I knew after that party it was time to move back home. Originally I left

Minnesota to escape the drugs. Now that I knew who had them in Florida, I knew it would only be a matter of time until I went back to being a full-fledged drug addict. I contemplated the decision for a few weeks, weighing my options. As far as I could see, I could stay and relive the horror story of addiction that brought me to Florida to begin with. I could lose my job, my house, my friends, my money, and my health. Or I could run away. I could go back home where I could have the support of my family while I tried to sort out the confusing pieces of my broken life.

My decision was clear. Once again I packed my bags, broke my lease and bought a one-way ticket. Only this time I was going home.

HOME SWEET HOME

Moving back to Minnesota after being gone for two years made for an interesting transition. Part of me felt like a failure because of all the chaos I got myself into in Florida. I missed my friends, my job, the warm weather and the life I'd built. Leaving a place always makes you realize how much people actually cared. My friends threw me a huge going away party. They all chipped in and bought me a case for my guitar and signed the case with really nice words to send me off. I still have that guitar case today.

I especially missed the church community I'd found in Florida, and I still had an inner sense of longing, searching, for something. I didn't know if I was trying to find myself, or God, or just some semblance of meaning in life. A friend of mine from high school was also searching for something deeper, so she and I visited a few churches. I also visited a church that my sister and her husband had started to attend. This was my first experience with a Pentecostal church. I was really confused as to why people were laying on the ground, weeping, and moaning in some other languages. I wondered if it was Arabic, or Hebrew, and I assumed that the people were super spiritual and once you were that deep in God you learned those other languages.

Later I discovered that those people were speaking in tongues, and that you can actually read about in the Bible. At the time, it was just a weird and slightly frightening experience that made me feel truly like an outsider. I determined never to return to that church again. It definitely wasn't the church for me!

My friend and I visited several churches and found one on the University of Minnesota campus that had a great vibe and a lot of young people. We attended there for a couple of months and then I found out that my friend was moving out of state for a while. I was really bummed to lose my church-hopping buddy but I was determined to keep going.

My sister invited me back to her church and I decided to take her up on the offer. After visiting so many other churches this one didn't seem so bad when I visited the second time. No one was weeping or speaking weird languages, and the messages that the pastor preached seemed to speak right to my heart.

One night I got invited out to eat with some of the young adults and the pastor. They seemed really cool, and although I felt somewhat different and inferior I tried to ignore it. I was just happy to be around new people who might become my good friends – friends who weren't into going out to bars and drinking and who had a sense of purpose and fullness. When the pastor asked me that night if I wanted to get involved in leadership I about fell out of my chair! Me? A church leader? Why would he ask that of me? I wasn't qualified. I wasn't even sober! I mean, I was sober that night when he asked me, but I wasn't planning on giving up drinking. I was only 22. I figured I had nothing to lose by saying yes to his offer. So I did.

I started showing up to Wednesday night youth group as a youth leader. Week after week I heard the Bible explained to middle school and high school students. It was exactly what I needed to learn the basics of Christianity. I began to read the Bible on my own and it was as if the words were leaping off the pages. I read it cover to cover. I kept finding answers to questions I didn't even know I had. The more I read, the more sense it made and I knew it was God I had been looking for all along - and that I was finding Him. I was excited about all my new knowledge but I also had a lot of questions. I was too embarrassed to ask them in youth group, so I often called my brother in law. I remember calling him to ask him what the difference was between God, Jesus, and the Holy Spirit, because sometimes I heard people praying to God and sometimes I heard them praying to Jesus. I thought I might be asked to pray sometime soon in youth group and I didn't want to mess up. I had many conversations with my brother in law about spiritual things. I was so thankful to have someone to talk to and answer all my questions.

This was a precious season in my life. I learned so much. I was able to attend leadership and discipleship classes with the rest of the church leaders. My passion for Jesus continued to grow. I was on a cloud.

Getting   involved   in   church   leadership

completely changed my life. It was much different than just showing up on a Sunday. I got to participate in something bigger than me, and it felt good. I had never experienced being a part of what God was doing. I'd heard about God and seen pictures of Jesus, but I didn't know that He actually spoke to us and worked through us. I didn't know that He was alive and real. At first I was still drinking alcohol here and there, but the closer I got to Jesus the less interested I was in feeling drunk.

Four months passed by and I hadn't taken a single drink. I was far more interested in singing worship music, reading the Bible, and hanging out with my new church friends. I had no idea how to be a youth leader, but looking back I see it was God's hand on my life orchestrating the circumstances so He could reveal Himself to me in the way that I could understand.

But one summer day, the sun was shining, the breeze was blowing the scent of fresh cut grass my way and a thought came to mind. "Wouldn't a beer be so refreshing?" Without hesitation I answered back to myself, "Mmm…yes!" I could almost taste it on my lips. I went out for a beer. It was delicious. It was refreshing. I only had one, and it didn't seem like a big deal. I thought God must have delivered me from alcoholism because I didn't feel the obsession to have a second drink.

But the next day I had another beer, and then another, and then a liter of vodka. I woke up with a terrible headache. After the fog wore off I wasn't sure who to talk to or what to do. I didn't know what it meant for my relationship with Jesus, my salvation, or my leadership position at church. I made the decision that I wouldn't tell anyone, and that it would never, ever happen again.

That plan didn't work so well for me. Secrets never bring us to health or wholeness. Sin, darkness, whatever you want to call it, it always takes us deeper than we want to go, for longer than we want to stay. The devil wants us to continue to keep our secrets because he knows that we are weaker when we're all alone.

Time went on and I continued drinking. I began to live a double life. I would get up on stage Sunday morning and lead worship, still drunk from the night before. I told everyone at church I was doing great. I could smile and say life was good but it was all a show. I was dying on the inside. Drowning in confusion, shame and guilt, I felt like I was being eaten alive by the double life I was living. Lies consumed every aspect of my life and I didn't know how long I could keep up the act. I desperately wanted to tell someone my secret, but I didn't know whom I could trust. I was afraid if I told someone at church that I'd get in trouble and get kicked out of leadership. I was afraid that my whole world would crumble and I'd lose all my friends as I had so many times before. I didn't want to have to run away again, skip town, and rebuild all over again because life had gotten so good this time. But alcohol had a hold on me and I was beginning to realize that no matter how hard I tried, I couldn't quit drinking. I didn't know what to do. Each time I drank I felt so disappointed in myself and I even felt disappointed in God. I thought He was so powerful and strong, and I didn't understand why He wouldn't set me free from my drinking habit.

You can only live two lives for so long. In the Bible it says that everything that is secret will eventually be brought into the open (Luke 8:17). Well, "eventually" came the hard way for me.

One night around Thanksgiving I went on a drinking binge. I had way too much alcohol, and once again I got behind the wheel. I got pulled over when I drove my car onto a bike path about 40 miles from my house. I have no idea how I got there. It's frightening to think how many times I've put myself, and others, in danger by driving while I was intoxicated. I'm so thankful that I never hurt anyone.

That night I went once again to spend the night in jail. Later I was charged with a second DUI and I was scared that people would read about it in the paper or hear about it on the news somehow, so I decided to confess to my pastor. I wanted him to hear it from me. I didn't want to show up to church and get blindsided by someone gossiping about my secret so I just came out with it one day in his office.

I was scared to death. I had never really told someone I looked up to about my problems. He was so kind and understanding, reassuring me that he and the church would be there to help me. The only problem was, I wasn't completely honest. I told him I got a DUI, as though it were a one time, "oops," and I didn't mention my life-controlling addiction to alcohol. As such, my pastor treated it as an isolated incident and we did some counseling to try to help me sort out my spiritual place in all of the confusion. I didn't lose any of my leadership privileges at that time because my pastor had the impression I had made a one-time mistake. He didn't know I was actually entangled in a really powerful addiction because I didn't tell him. My drinking was completely out of control. When I started, I couldn't stop. I always needed another drink, and another, and another, until I blacked out.

Things continued to get darker for me. One day I started drinking early in the morning knowing youth group would be happening later that night. I thought I could just drink a few shots of vodka and stop an hour or two before youth group, drink some coffee, and be good to go. But the hours kept passing, and the shots kept coming. I was completely wasted when my dad dropped me off at youth group. I don't remember exactly what happened that night – but whatever I did or said made it obvious to my youth pastor that I was heavily intoxicated.

I went to church the next Sunday with my church face on, hiding my fear and shame, and hoping that I could just avoid making eye contact with anyone – especially my pastor. No one said a word to me about what had happened and I started to wonder if maybe I hadn't made as big a scene as I thought previously. Then after service, my pastor pulled me aside and confronted me. Like a dog with its tail between its legs, I sheepishly confessed. I couldn't deny it. He told me that I was no longer going to be able to stay in leadership. I couldn't be a youth leader and I couldn't' sing on the worship team. I continued in counseling, but after a few more sessions and my honest confession that I hadn't been able to stay sober he strongly recommended that I go to treatment. He suggested a program called Teen Challenge.

When I looked into the program and realized it was an entire year long I was mortified. I didn't want to have to quit my job and move into a treatment house for a whole year! But I thought long and hard about it and decided to go. I felt a sense of relief that this would be the hard end to my drinking, and a year was a small price to pay for the many years I'd already handed over to the god of addiction.

Many details needed to be worked out as I prepared to leave my entire life behind and live in an inpatient treatment center for the next year of my life. I loved my job at a small non-profit, and my boss was shocked to hear that I was resigning because I had an alcohol problem and needed to go to rehab. I was very good at living as a functional alcoholic and no one at work suspected I had a drinking problem. I'd called in sick a couple more times than average but while I was there I did high quality work. Willing to do whatever I needed to do to kill the beast of addiction that was living inside of me, I put my job and the rest of my life on hold to try to deal with my problem once and for good. I had no idea what God had in store for me in the year to come.

REHAB

I think the old adage is true in so many ways: you never know what you've got until it's gone. I believe the same principle can be applied to suffering in that you don't always realize just how bad it is until things start to get better. I had no idea how much my addiction was suffocating me until I walked through the doors of Teen Challenge and began to be able to breathe again. I had no idea just how sick I was until I started to get well.

Slowly but surely the darkness began to be drowned out by the light. Surrounded by amazing staff, leaders, teachers and counselors, I had an army around me cheering me on to victory and sobriety. There were so many other women in the program with such powerful testimonies of God's faithfulness and deliverance. Hearing their stories gave me hope that I could have a happy ending too. Freedom was everywhere. And for the first time in a long time I had hope. I was growing closer to Jesus every day. His word once again came alive to me as I memorized countless scriptures. Prayer became a foundational part of my day. As my understanding of God grew, so did my dependence upon Him. Faith became real to me. No longer enigmatic or fleeting, my faith became tangible, applicable, and functional. I began to know Jesus as my very best friend, my healer, my comforter, my rock, and my deliverer. These things may not make sense to you if you're not a follower of Christ, but the instant you make a decision to trust Him, He begins to reveal Himself to you in a way a that makes sense to you. He did it for me, and I have no doubt in my mind He will do it for you too if you just simply ask.

At Teen Challenge I experienced freedom from so much more than just drugs and alcohol. As part of the healing process, I received educated on the impact of drugs and alcohol and I began to see my addiction as more of a symptom of deeper issues and not as the root of the problem. Spiritual counseling uncovered childhood hurts I didn't even realize I had and helped me to begin the process of healing from years of damaged emotions. I had no idea that lurking underneath my addiction were insecurity, pride, abandonment, rejection, and fear, woven into a tangled tapestry with the help of a skillful enemy who wanted my life and soul. I began to understand that God was for me, and Satan was against me, and life on this side of eternity is an all-out war. Teen Challenge was a place of refuge for me to safely sort out my pain without the ability to turn to alcohol and drugs to cope. I can't tell you how heavy a weight lifted off my shoulders when I faced all my baggage and actually processed through it. I gave myself permission to feel, to grieve, to forgive others who'd hurt me, and to forgive myself for all the choices I'd made in my addiction. And most importantly, I learned the grace of God meant that Jesus forgave me for all that I'd done. It was hard for me to fully grasp that I could just have a clean slate, and the hardest part was forgiving myself. But I did it.

Another great thing about Teen Challenge was that there were opportunities within the program for women who displayed leadership qualities to grow in their capacity to lead. I'll never forget the day when the program director told me she saw me as a leader. I had the opportunity to serve in some student-leadership positions during my time at Teen Challenge. The director spent time with those of us in leadership roles, teaching us great lessons about life and leadership. About half way through my month program I got some bad news. I found out that our program director was leaving. She had accepted a position in New York City and I was absolutely devastated. I looked up to her so much, and I felt connected to her. I trusted her. To my absolute surprise, she told me that there was one internship position available with her at the women's center in New York and she invited me to come work for her when I graduated the program. I couldn't believe it! I was honored. There were so many students in the program, and there was only one internship available. And she picked me. I told her I would take her up on her offer. But something inside told me she'd change her mind by the time I actually graduated and not to get my hopes up because I didn't trust that people actually meant what they said and followed through. Sure enough, the end of my program drew near and I had multiple options. I was also offered an internship with the Prevention department. I'd spent several days volunteering with Prevention during my time in the program and loved it. We'd go into schools

and talk to students about the risks and consequences of substance abuse and share our personal
stories of addiction. I loved sharing my story and I
discovered my gift of speaking through that
experience.

My previous employer said they'd take me back
in a heartbeat and that if there was no open position available, they'd create one for me. Teen Challenge also had a ministry school option where
graduates of the program could go to transition and
continue to grow deeper in their faith. I had several
viable options. I knew I had a difficult decision
to make.

Right around the last month or so of my
program began the haunting. I began to feel a
strong urge and desire to drink alcohol again. Daily
it seemed, a glass of wine would appear in my mind
shimmering in its splendor. I didn't tell a single soul.
It was my secret to keep. After all, if Teen Challenge had a poster child, it was me. If anyone was
to look at my graduating class and guess who would
be "most likely to succeed," I would've been at the
top of that list. Maybe it was because I'd had a
genuinely life-changing experience with God.
Maybe it was because my gifts of singing and
speaking became so apparent through the program.

Those shiny, platform gifts require character; and while I had made some major improvements in that year, I still had a long way to go.

Pride was a major struggle for me. So I planned my relapse long before it ever happened. I tucked it away in the farthest corner of my mind and I took the job in New York City. I figured I'd relapse eventually but at least I could be far enough away that most of the people who thought I was amazing and gifted wouldn't have to see me or wouldn't find out I had gone back to my old ways.

New York was intimidating to say the least. I was 25 years old, a suburban Minnesota "nice" girl, moving all alone to the big city. I knew exactly one person there - my mentor and now boss. It didn't take long for me to feel incredibly lonely and lost in a really big city, surrounded by people who all seemed to know exactly who they were and where they were going. I was so intimidated when I tried going to small groups and people asked why I'd moved to New York. They were actors and models and lawyers and med students. And my greatest accomplishment was I'd just graduated rehab. I felt so small. I was ashamed of my story. I couldn't connect and be myself.

On top of the loneliness there was the allure of

the New York City nightlife. I'd partied in Minnesota and Florida and had so much fun, but I couldn't imagine what it'd be like to party in this city. I worked for a non-profit in New York which was located in the really posh, expensive area on the Upper East Side. As a staff member, I lived on site. Our building was within walking distance of so many cool looking bars and pubs. I'd walk by and see beautiful and sophisticated looking people in there and I'd imagine myself being their friend.

No longer in the safety of a controlled and scheduled spiritual environment, I started spending less time with God. There was so much to see and explore in New York, and now I had to work full time. I didn't have a ton of free time and I found myself not wanting to spend it with God. My interest in reading His word and prayer declined. I just wasn't all that interested in Him anymore, as the world began to look a whole lot more exciting.

One night I was sitting at a coffee shop reading a magazine and a man walked by the window. He was attractive. I noticed him. And seconds later, he was sitting next to me in Starbucks. He was charming and as we started chatting, I found out he was from Chicago. We bonded over stories of Midwestern life and he told me he'd come out to

New York to be a lawyer. We hit it off. I didn't tell him much about my story, but I felt comfortable enough to be myself. He got my number and I was excited to make a friend. His life was way different than mine. He worked for a busy attorney in the big city. He lived in the fast lane. He went out to eat every night and drank and had a fancy apartment in the city. We started hanging out a lot, and my feelings for him grew. I was torn because I knew I shouldn't be spending so much time with someone who drank. He wasn't an alcoholic. But I knew I needed my closest friends to be people who were running after God and who knew my history. But I dismissed all of that because we had such a genuine connection and I loved spending time with him. He was a good guy and he made me laugh. He told me stories about him drinking with his friends and partying until late hours in the night. I told him I didn't really drink – but that's *all* I told him. I didn't mention rehab or my drug addiction or my alcohol problems. I think he thought I was just a goody two shoes kind of girl who didn't drink. It was only a matter of time until I had a drink.

At first, I just had one or two drinks here and there. I remembered the buzz and warm feeling. Nothing had changed. But within weeks of taking that first drink I was drinking alone blacking out again.

I wrestled because I desperately wanted to be a social drinker, and I didn't think it was fair that I couldn't just have a glass of wine with dinner. The problem wasn't alcohol. The problem was my addiction. Once again, it had a hold on my life. I was no longer in control. I was living a lie. I had a lot of questions as to what this relapse meant for my spiritual life. Had the last year of my life been a waste? Had I abandoned God? Could I come back to Him after having such an experience and walking away?

Darkness and depression began to flood my soul and my life became confusing. I was working in Christian ministry, teaching women about princi-ples for living a godly life, freedom and discipleship and I was the biggest hypocrite of all with my secrets. I kept telling myself I could just quit. But I couldn't. I was so afraid of being judged and condemned by God and I could feel a heavy burden of darkness upon my life. The darkness was isolat-ing. Sheer evil, it daily beckoned me deeper into the doldrums of depression, reminding me of how far I'd fallen from God, and convincing me I was too far gone to turn back towards Him. I began to sink deeper.

I spent most nights blacked out in the parks of New York City, asking people where I could find meth. Everyone in New York did heroine. It was impossible to find meth. Then one night during a blackout I somehow found meth again. I think someone gave me acid or some other drug. I'm not sure, but it was a very fuzzy night for me. But I woke up, took the train home, and I was supposed to work that morning.

I felt like death and I couldn't keep up the act any more. I knew I couldn't call in sick to work without my boss taking one look at me and seeing the relapse all over my face. Rather than lie, I put my keys in the front door, and walked straight up to the 4th floor to my boss' office. I must've looked like death itself. I confessed everything; my drug relapse the night before and how I'd been secretly drinking. She looked at me with eyes of compassion in a way that no human had ever looked at me before. With tears in her eyes she said she was so sorry I'd been going through that. She told me I could no longer keep the internship and I'd have a few days to make a plan and move out.

I expected her to yell at me and tell me I was

stupid. But in her eyes I saw grace and love. I saw Jesus. It was hard for me to accept the consequence that I'd lost my job and would have to move but I knew I couldn't bargain or manipulate. I'd just have to accept it.

I told my guy-friend the truth about my story and how I was getting kicked out. He felt so bad that I was going through all of it, and wanted to help. We tried to figure out a way for me to stay in New York. He even offered for me to live with him. But I knew my addiction had gotten really out of hand and I had no idea what to expect because I couldn't trust myself to go a single day without drinking and doing something foolish.

The next few years went by as a bit of a blur. I didn't want to leave New York. I was in and out of a few other treatment centers. But in my heart I truly didn't want to change. I didn't want to be in treatment. I wanted to make it in New York. I dropped out of treatment and tried getting a job and an apartment and picking up the pieces of my life. I moved around a lot. The only constant in my life was alcohol, and I kept trying to find meth in New York but people were really only into cocaine and heroine. Eventually I surrendered to the fact that New York City was a beast and had swallowed me whole. I felt like such a failure getting on that plane back to Minnesota. I was hopeless and homeless, and I went to the one place where I knew God had met me before. I prayed He would meet me again at Minnesota Teen Challenge Once again, I was greeted with grace and love. My desire to change was growing, but I still wasn't completely ready to give up on the idea of being a social drinker. Shame, guilt, and disappointment brought hardness to my heart. I was mostly in treatment because I needed a roof over my head long enough to escape the brutal winter and I was not really interested in sobriety. I put on a good enough show and followed the rules closely enough not to get caught. But I was only cheating myself. I had moments of healing and wanting change, but I had more moments of wanting to go back to drinking. The battle between darkness and light raged on. Every day it seemed a different side was gaining ground, and I was torn.

JOURNAL ENTRY. SOMETIME AFTER I LEFT NEW YORK AND RETURNED TO TEEN CHALLENGE FOR TREATMENT. THIS JOURNAL WAS WRITTEN WHILE I WAS IN TEEN CHALLENGE:

Dear God,

I come to you now in Jesus name. Lord, thank you for restoring my feelings. Today I felt anxious, surprised, relieved, and thankful. The best feeling was thankful. Lord, I've been living in this apathy and it bothers me. I want to be the kind of person who is joyful. I want to be filled with your joy and smiles and laughter. But I can't fake it. I feel like the mood stabilizer medication I am on makes me a zombie and I want to get off it. I plan to. God, I want to be that type of person that other people can go to for help. I want to be dependable, consistent, wise, gentle yet firm, loving, and truly humble. A servant, a student of your word. Please mold me into these things most of all Lord. I give you every desire for personal glory. I repent of wanting the glory all for myself. I give you all the glory, honor, and praise. Let my life point to you…

I can't remember the names and locations of all the different treatment centers I went to over the next few years. Alcohol had the strongest hold on me and despite all the drama and chaos it brought into my life, I didn't want to give it up. In between relapses, I'd get a great job, go back to school, and find a church. Life would improve, but it would never last. Depression began to take an even stronger grip on my life. I wanted to die so often during those days. My life felt so meaningless and it seemed like I failed at everything. I failed at being sober. I failed at getting drunk. I couldn't drink responsibly. I couldn't keep anything stable in my life. I wasn't sure if God had abandoned me, or if He hated me or was punishing me. I thought about ending my life almost every day.

JOURNAL ENTRY. SOMETIME IN BETWEEN TREATMENTS:

Suicide. If I were to do it, I'd buy a really nice white dress. A wedding dress. And a gun. And plenty of pills. I mean if I'm gonna do it I'm gonna … do it. The only reason I didn't kill myself today is because I am not fully convinced I'd spend eternity in heaven. I'm scared to go to hell. But life is hell. I already live in constant torment so I'm not sure how much worse the real hell could actually be. I suppose this life does have its moments of relief, but they never last. The depression has gotten so bad that I can't do my job. People look at me and I guess they see greatness, or potential. Funny, I see filth. I see failure. I see someone who will never win. I desperately want to fall asleep. Forever. I just want to die. When I close my eyes I see visions of my bloody hands grasping at a wall. Realizing I'm about to actually die, I suddenly have regret. I suddenly want to live as I see a flickering vision of what life might have been. But it is too late. My heart strains to beat, my lungs gasp for their final breath. In an instant, my soul leaves my body, and my misery comes to an end. I have peace, and I do not have to suffer anymore....

Thankfully I never let my suicidal thoughts get the best of me. I didn't really have anyone to talk to about it, but I wrote in my journal often to get my feelings out of my head and writing helped me process what I was experiencing.

I just could not stop drinking. Alcohol helped me to cope with my heavy emotions. I'd be feeling sad and depressed one moment, and as soon as I would drink a little bit, I'd feel better. I felt normal again. I didn't feel as defeated, and I remembered that I was capable of laughing and smiling. The problem was, once I started drinking, I couldn't stop. One or two drinks made me feel normal. Three or four drinks gave me a decent buzz. And five or six drinks put me right on my way to eight or nine, which led me to blackouts. They say alcohol lowers your inhibitions. I couldn't agree more. I did really stupid things when I had too much to drink. Careless, dangerous things, that I would never have done sober. One night I was on social media after drinking alone for several hours. I found a guy I knew of as a drug dealer when I was into meth after high school. I sent him a private message and within 30 minutes there was a black BMW convertible in my driveway. A beautiful, meth-skinny girl drove me to a cheap hotel and fifteen minutes later I had a needle in my arm. I shot meth again for the first time in years. It took my breath away. I absolutely loved it.

JOURNAL ENTRY. SHORTLY AFTER THE NIGHT I RELAPSED ON METH, AROUND AGE 27:

You probably wouldn't believe me if I told you where I am and what I am doing. I drove to Brooklyn Park, got a hotel, and now I'm sitting here alone. I'm so high. And I have so much dope left. I wish he'd given me less. Well I say that now as I'm shaking and my eyes can't quite catch the lines on the page. I should've slept first. Of course I didn't sleep last night. Now I am missing work. I'm out with the "flu." My arms look just terrible. They're all marked up because I've been using the same needle for three days. I wouldn't just humble myself and go buy some (finally I did). I got drunk last Friday, which is how this whole big mess got started. I sent a FaceBook message to a drug dealer to hang out, and it'd been a while but same old, same old. Crazy, right? I just let this kid draw something on my back and it turned out to be fabulous so I let him ink up my entire back. It's a tree with some sick winding roots and then some wings. Well, one wing. He took a smoke break and never came back so he'll have to finish it another day. Maybe today. Who knows. I could see what He's up tp. Maybe I could give him the last of my dope so I don't have to deal with it anymore. I'm all paranoid driving. Plus I'm not eating. I'm a freaking twig and I don't like it. I can't believe my size 2 pants are kind of too big for me. Well, in my defense, I am a runner. Man, how did I get here? Bloodstains? Lies? Double – life? I need to rewind back to when things were going well and examine exactly what happened to lead me up to this point...

ROCK BOTTOM

I still remember the day I turned the car around on that city street. I'd been doing enough meth on and off that I could still make it through the work day without any withdrawal symptoms on the days I wasn't using. But on this day I knew that as I was driving home I should just go home. Because at that point if I'd turned the car around and headed toward the dope house to pick up, I knew I would be officially crossing the line from casual use to addiction, and at that point I would need to be high in order to stay awake through the work day. Meth withdrawals make you very, very tired. Like narcoleptic tired. You can just fall asleep at any moment. Wrestling with my soul, I went back and forth between going home and going to get high for several blocks until the drugs finally won. Both reluctantly and excitedly I turned the car around. I could not wait to get high that night!

Life once again began the descent in the downward spiral that is meth addiction. Like they say in Narcotics Anonymous and Alcoholics Anonymous, the road always leads to the same place – jails, institutions, and death. This time around for me was worse than any hell on earth I could ever imagine. They say when you relapse you pick up where you left off and things get worse. Fast. I believe it. I lived it. So much so that to this day I believe with all my heart that if I was to start using again, I'd be dead within a month. It just can't get any worse than my last relapse, apart from death itself.

First, it was the panic attacks. I used to think panic attacks were ridiculous. Pure fiction. Something girls in rehab did to get attention and make people feel sorry for them or get them some prescription drugs to calm them down. I'd sit alone with my needles, shooting drugs into my veins, and instead of getting high, panic would take over my mind and body. I was usually alone so I would just try to contain it, writing in my journal, but I would start to believe I was having a heart attack and I would stop being able to breathe. Over and over I was faced with the reality that I could possibly die.

As often as I'd think about how much I just wanted to die, staring death in the face gave me cold feet. I was petrified. Typically, I'd call 911 and say I thought I was having an overdose. An ambulance would come, I'd say I flushed the drugs, they'd bring me to the hospital and pump some sort of downer drug into my system to calm me down and slow my heart rate. They'd do an EKG and tell me my heart did not suffer a heart attack, that it was a panic attack. And I would believe my fears and my feelings over the doctors. It felt like a heart attack to me.

Every time this happened I would lay there in the hospital, knowing there was no friend or family member I should call to come get me and no home to go back to. I felt so frustrated that my life had come to this point. I knew I was getting closer to death. I thought back to my old boyfriend who'd passed away from a drug overdose. He was mixing meth and heroin—uppers and downers—because when he'd shoot up meth he was getting to the point of panic attacks, so unless he mixed in some heroine, the high wasn't an enjoyable experience for him. Over time, mixing the uppers and downers caused his heart to weaken, and then one time he took a regular dose of drugs, but because of his heart being weakened, it became a fatal dose and he died.

I wasn't living in Minnesota at the time but I'm sure when he died, it was alone, in a room, with a needle in his arm. I thought of this every time I went to the ER and they pumped me full of downers. I was slipping away and I wondered if this would be my fate too. I thought about the impact this would have on my family, who would come to my funeral, and what people would say about me. I wondered if I would die with a needle in my arm, a prodigal daughter astray from God, a laughing stock in the pit of hell as Satan and all his demons clapped hands for the win. I wondered if I did actually die, would I go to heaven or hell? I wasn't completely sure. I can't tell you what terrified me more - death, or the fact that I didn't know the answer to that question.

JOURNAL ENTRY. A POEM WRITTEN WHILE HIGH ON METH. ORIGINALLY ENTITLED, "CAGED." CAGED WAS CROSSED OUT AND REPLACED WITH, "STOCKHOLM SYNDROME":

This double life brings no sleep in the night
  Got me crawling in darkness but calling it light
  Hopelessly search as I seek satisfaction

But these demons to me have become a distraction
Somehow in the midst of a fatal attraction
I've become someone I'd never imagine
Tormented and chained just a corpse in a cage
Enchanted by my captor's devious ways
Someday I'll break away, just not today
But I chose this path, I'm the one to be blamed
I'm trying to fight but this war is relentless
Gave my life to this high but I just can't defend it.
I am hopeless, devoted, and fully dependent.

———

Lost and tormented by the ever-growing addiction to meth, darkness consumed my life. The consequences of using drugs are in no way unpredictable. Everything that happens to drug addicts as their life slips away was happening to me. I'd emptied my bank account, lost my job, got kicked out of my sober house, and was living in my car. Summer was winding down and a cooler autumn was settling in and I knew it was time to act. Winter in Minnesota is brutally cold and I wouldn't survive living in my car for the winter. On top of that, I was getting tired. In AA and NA they call it, "sick and tired of being sick and tired." Every day, every moment, I really felt like I might die today or tomorrow if I don't get sober. Each time I stuck a needle in my arm I did it with the fear and hesitation that it could quite possibly stop my heart and end my life. It was no longer fun. I was just very, very sick. Each time I'd get high I was convinced I was going to die, so I would write notes in my journal, hoping someone would find them and know that I wasn't trying to kill myself. I was just a drug addict, and I wanted my family to know I was sorry for the life I'd lived. I wanted them to know that it was not their fault and I didn't want them to blame themselves. Just in case I actually died from the meth, alone in a hotel room, I didn't want them to wonder. After countless hospital stays, and too many days feeling like I was on the brink of death, I started to toy with the idea of trying treatment one more time.

I don't know why I went back. I don't know where I found the strength or the sanity to make that phone call and get myself back into Teen Challenge–but I did. This would be my tenth and final treatment.

When the day came to actually check myself in, I was hesitant. Getting sober meant cutting ties forever with my best friend. Meth was my constant companion, my source of life, my god. Reluctantly I checked myself into treatment. I had no idea what to expect.

The first few days were a whirlwind. It took a while for the drugs to leave my system, and before I crashed in withdrawal, I can only describe my state of mind as a drug induced psychosis. I had an elaborate suicide note written in the front of my journal and I kept walking around showing it to the staff and asking if they were going to come to my funeral.

*Journal entry. Suicide brainstorm session, written shortly before going to treatment for the last time. I brought this note around to people in treatment to ask them if they would go to my funeral. (**Caution:** This is VERY graphic.):*

Suicide Brainstorm session. Timeframe: Sometime between now and Halloween. Don't want Christmas to be a reminder. Things to do before I die: write the letter, grow my nails out and get a French manicure.

Possible methods:

- *Intentional overdose (need money to buy*

> *drugs/need to charge my phone/pick a place/write note?/buy a new dress/closed casket due to bloating?/what if I don't actually die and I only have a stroke and then I'm stuck in a wheelchair for the rest of my life?)*

- *Shoot myself in the head (need money to buy a gun/closed casket) **I really want an open casket to give my friends and family a better chance at getting closure.*
- *Hang myself (not sure how to tie a noose or where I'd hang myself from since I am homeless)*
- *Classic wrist slit (where would I find a sharp enough knife? This would ruin my nice outfit)*

Hesitations: Not sure I'll go to heaven. But life is hell already anyway. This might hurt some people. Oh well. If they cared so much they'd have shown it while I was alive.

At one point the staff had to call in the Peace Officers, who hauled me off to the psych ward for an evaluation to be sure I wasn't suicidal to the point where it was unsafe for me to remain in the program.

This wasn't my first time being put in a psychiatric ward. I was locked away in a padded room, and stripped of everything that could potentially be a suicide hazard. They took my shoelaces, my necklace, and my bracelets. I sat there for days eating hospital food when they brought it and waiting for the doctors to evaluate me. I think I began to come to my senses while I was there. I suddenly felt so strongly that I did not need to live a life anymore that put me in places like psych wards and jail.

Loud screams and pounding sounds were coming from the rooms around me and if I looked out my door when it opened, I saw people in really, really bad shape coming through the halls to smoke or use the bathroom. I remember thinking, "I don't belong here." A war raged on in inside of me. Light and darkness, angels and demons, and heaven and hell all battled to have the final say over what to do with my lost soul. Caught between the idea of life and death, vacillating in the hope of one or the other coming soon because the valley of indecision was swallowing me whole.

Seventy-two hours later I was cleared by the doctors and released back to the program to complete my treatment. By this time the drugs had worn off completely and I was feeling a myriad of emotion. Shame, confusion, hopelessness, and despair flooded my heart and mind, competing for the throne. I glanced in the mirror in my rehab bedroom and looked upon the face of an absolute stranger. Eyes void of life and a vacant smile, I pitied her. She was pitiful. I was pitiful.

Something broke inside of me. The last little piece of my hope and my will to live shattered. At that moment I gave myself over to death. I was finally defeated. I sat down on the edge of my bed counting the things I had to live for and came up with zero. I'd lost everything.

This doesn't seem like the typical way to set a stage for a miracle moment. But God does not do things in a typical way. He is not a typical God.

Without realizing I was doing it, I began to pray. Words flooded out from my lips. I wasn't crying out to God to ask him to save me or to help me. I thought about everything I knew about the Bible, Jesus, and my life. I pleaded with the Lord. I didn't want help and I didn't want a rescue. I wanted death and I wanted it immediately. I told God how I know that the Bible says in the book of Deuteronomy that "today I have placed before you life and death. Choose life." Desperate I recited that verse to the Lord and told Him that I didn't want to choose life. I'd lost everything and I was tired of losing. My life had been shattered ten times over and I didn't have it in me to even think about beginning the process of picking up the pieces one more time. I didn't even have the slightest hope that it was possible. I was hopeless. I poured out my argument before Him. I stated my case. My only hope was that He would see my hopelessness and reward me with death. I was at my lowest. I begged God to please, please, just let me die.

I paused to wait for His response, almost certain I felt relief that he was going to allow me to just fall asleep and die. His words pierced through the darkness of my soul with a light so bright, words cannot express. At first when He whispered, "*I still have hope in you,*" it was so quiet and still, I almost had to lean forward to see if I'd really heard anything. Then once more I heard Him speak, a bit louder this time. "I still have hope in you." These six words would change my life for all eternity. It wasn't an audible voice, but I heard it so tangibly inside my soul, it felt audible to me. I was astonished. The God of the Universe, the one who created the heavens and the earth and who holds it all together, the one who tells the ocean, "this far and no further shall you go," *that* God would reach down from His holy hill and speak to me in my darkest, dirtiest, most desperate moment.

From that moment on something changed in me from the inside out. It was like a light that had been off was switched on again and I knew I had been set free. I never returned to meth and have been drug free since that day. As I am writing this I am coming upon five years without alcohol, drugs, or cigarettes. I have shared this story countless times to thousands of people, and when I get to the part where I heard Him speak, it's as though it happened just yesterday. I had an encounter with the living God. It was a divine experience. I believe God wants to touch not only my life, but the lives of all His people. Whether they have been living for Him or not. He is after our hearts.

That was a life changing moment for me. I will never forget it. I didn't think I was actually capable of living free of drugs and alcohol. I wanted death because life was too much work, too full of disappointment, and for me it had become hopeless. God heard my cry but answered me with life instead of death. I had no idea what a beautiful future he had in store for me in the days and years ahead.

God has done so much in my life since that miracle moment where He spoke to me in my bed at treatment. God has opened the door for me to share my story and to impact many people across the nation. But it's not my story. It's God's story. I just showed up. God has given me a wonderful husband, a healthy baby boy (and another baby on the way), wonderful friendships, a great church home, peace of mind, restoration in my relationships, and so many opportunities to be a good neighbor and to help others in need. He has done great things for me and some day, at the end of my life, I will see Him face to face and be with Him forever in eternity.

I share my story because I believe that there are people out there who think God could never love them because of what they've done. Trust me, my friend, God has so much more love than we could ever begin to understand in our limited human minds. I promise you that if you ask God to forgive you, He will. If you invite Jesus to just walk with you, and you learn what it means to follow Him, it will be a decision you will never regret. God changes lives. Impossible lives. Broken lives. Messy lives. Ugly, shameful, tattered lives - He restores and heals.

The Bible has so much to offer in helping us to know God more. One of my favorite chapters is

Romans 8. In it, Paul the Apostle tells us that we are "more than conquerors." I've thought about what that might mean so often. I've wondered why he didn't just call us "conquerors" or "victors." But to be *more* than a conqueror, what does that mean?

One person I consider a hero in my faith journey is Christine Caine. We've never met, but I heard her explain this verse and it resonated to the deepest core of my being. She said, *"to be more than a conqueror means that not only have you overcome, but you're now letting God use your story to help others."* That's so powerful.

Friend, if you are reading this today, I believe God has a message for you. No matter what you're going through, God can heal you and allow that same trial to be a tool to help bring healing to other hurting people around you. The way He does things is often not the way we would have chosen or designed. It doesn't mean things won't be messy and ugly and painful and difficult. But He will be with us in the mess. But He is big and wise and full of love. His desire is to set us free and to use our influence to help others! You are not defeated! You can overcome. You are more than a conqueror!

A FINAL NOTE FROM PORCIA

I can't begin to thank you enough for reading my story! I give all the credit to my wonderful Jesus, who carried me through my darkest moments. He loved me enough to die for me. I can't even begin to grasp that some days.

I shared a lot of very personal and raw material in this book, especially from my old journals. I hope that seeing just how dark my darkness was allowed you to develop a greater understanding of the power of Christ to set us free.

If you or anyone you know is having thoughts of suicide, please reach out to someone immediately. There are people who will help and resources to get you through. Suicide is NOT the answer. If there is no one you can think of to call or text, no parent, teacher, friend, or youth pastor, please call

911 or the National Suicide Prevention Line at 1-800-273-8255. Or you can chat with them online. Suicide can be prevented. Your life is worth so much more than you know. You don't have to go through this alone.

The next few pages contain stories from several of my friends. I hope you will enjoy reading about their experiences and victories! Their stories are different than mine. Their struggles are different than mine. But what we all have in common is that we clung to Jesus and allowed Him to bring us through our trials, and now we are allowing Him to use what we've been through to help and influence others and to build the Kingdom of Christ! Feel free to get in touch with any of my friends if their stories impact you. I'm sure they will love to hear from you!

On Mission,
Porcia

NORA'S STORY

I remember that moment so clearly. The shame. The guilt. I hated myself and I promised I would never, ever do it again. It was about 15 years ago and I was on a missions trip to Guatemala with some other people from my church. After a busy morning of volunteering at a construction site, someone ordered pizza for the group and we all took a break to eat.

I took a slice, then another, and then another. I wasn't counting. If I had to guess, I'd probably eaten about six or seven slices when a one of the guys (who was about three times my size) said, "Wow! You sure know how to put down a pizza!" I didn't really give it much thought. I was just eating how I would have eaten if I were alone. As lunch was wrapping up, I watched the pastor's wife take a box of pizza and put it over by a shed. It was Baseball Game Pizza – with mustard, and hot dogs. Yuck. I absolutely hate mustard. But I couldn't stop obsessing over it. We were supposed to be working and all I could think about was a way to get over to that pizza without anyone seeing me.

Sure enough, everyone went over to the other side of the work site. "Now was my only chance," I thought to myself as I bolted to make a mad dash for the pizza. I ate the entire thing. I hated every second of it. I stuffed bite after bite into my mouth, eating as fast as I could so that no one would find out. A few minutes after I rejoined the group at the work site the pastor showed up. He must've been away doing some work and he hadn't had a chance to eat. His wife had set aside that box of pizza for him. I heard him walk up to his wife and say, "Honey, I'm starving. I haven't eaten all day. Did you save me some of my favorite Baseball Game Pizza?"

My heart sank.

I felt so ashamed. I didn't enjoy it. I wasn't physically hungry. I hated myself and I made a promise to myself that I would never do it again. And I kept that promise. Until three hours later.

This was my life. Promise made. Promise

broken. Try harder. Do better. Failed diets. Constantly going back and forth. God, help me. I would cry out to God asking him to set me free from the desire to constantly put food into my body but it seemed my cries were going unheard. I would drive my car past neon fast food signs and think to myself, "Just go home." But then I'd see a sign at Baker's Square that said, "Free Pie after 5 pm," and I couldn't help but stop. On my way back I'd see a McDonald's drive through and try to resist. But I needed just one Hot Apple Pie. Then I'd go through the drive through and find out they were two for $1. With all of my strength I wanted to say no to that drive through cashier asking me if I wanted two, but I couldn't resist. I'd drive with my knees so I could use both hands to get the scalding hot apple pies into my mouth as fast as I could because I had to scarf it down. Food was my drug.

I would lie in bed every night grabbing at the excess fat on my arms and my stomach. I woke up every morning with a new resolution. I'd have egg whites for breakfast and be so proud of myself for being strong. Then by 4 pm I'd blow it. I'd get donuts or cookies or candy and try again tomorrow.

Fast forward to February 19th, nine years ago. It was the last day I consumed sugar. It was after

Valentine's Day so the grocery store I was shopping at had this huge cart of chocolate and candy marked at 75% off. I should have walked away as soon as I spotted it, but it beckoned me. It knew my name. I bought almost the entire cart full of nearly expired candy. With my adrenaline pumping I went home in anticipation of getting my fix. I walked in my house, closed all the curtains, and sat on the far side of the living room on the floor so no one could see me. Because I have always been a calorie counter, I can tell you that on that particular afternoon I consumed about 7,000 calories worth of Valentine's candy. My body started sweating. My heart was pounding. I thought I was going to have a heart attack and on that day, I knew that I needed help.

I didn't know where to start but I knew I needed something. I mean, I was a Christian. I went to church. I read my Bible. I listened to worship music. I just didn't know how to find the help I needed. I had a friend who'd been struggling with alcoholism who had to spend some time in jail for a DUI. He actually met a pastor during his time in jail and after he got out he attended a recovery ministry group at the pastor's church. My friend invited me to come along to the meeting and I accepted.

I had no idea this was God actually directing my steps and leading me to the help I needed. At the meeting, the worship music was really good, and I loved the message. Of course, I wasn't an alcoholic or a drug addict, but I still felt like a lot of what was said applied to me. I happened to pick up a flyer at the church and noticed another meeting listed. "Food Addicts Victorious." Tuesdays at 7 pm. I was surprised. I had no idea that food addiction was something people talked about. I was instantly drawn to the idea of this meeting. I knew I needed to go. But I was scared. I wondered what would happen if I showed up and everyone was significantly larger than me and they'd look at me like I didn't belong. I was scared they'd think I didn't really have a problem and wouldn't take me seriously. But I decided to go anyway.

There were three people at the meeting. One was larger than me and one was smaller. They shared what they did in secret and I realized I was not alone. I felt so much peace and relief just to know someone else had been through what I was going through and made it out to the other side. They were walking in victory. I knew I would not have to have this problem for the rest of my life. I also knew that change would require hard work, but I was ready. I was desperate.

I changed a lot of things about my lifestyle and I avoided certain social situations for a while when I first got "clean." Sugar was a drug for me, and because it created such a sense of craving for me I knew I had to abstain from it completely. The fact that others had successfully managed to give up sugar altogether inspired me to have hope that I could do it too. I'm happy to say that today I have nine years clean from my addiction to processed sugar!

The journey of getting clean was full of some confusing moments. But I'm grateful that God allowed this trial in my life for many reasons. The world is a hurting place, and pain relates. I feel like I can have so much more compassion on people who are struggling with addiction because I know what it's like to hate what you're doing but not be able to stop. One person in particular who has struggled in my life is my husband. When we met, he was a worship leader working in full time ministry. We fell in love, got married, and he relapsed six months later. After three years of mass destruction and living in active addiction, his choices led him to a courtroom and the judge sentenced him to 75 months in prison. That's six years! This was not the way I thought my fairytale Christian marriage would go. But because of what I've been through, I have been able to have so much compassion toward my husband. I've been able to stay married, be his cheerleader, and be the best wife that I can be as God is working in him.

Nora currently works in natural healthcare at a nutritional education center. She volunteers with addiction recovery ministries. If you are suffering with food addiction, she recommends you look into Overeaters Anonymous online, and find a local or virtual meeting for support. Many churches also have a program called Celebrate Recovery, where many breakout groups also address food addiction.

MARK'S STORY

Don't throw in the towel before you taste victory! My name is Mark Chatman, although I was born Christopher Johnson Powell. Born into an unstable home, my biological mother struggled with drug addiction for several years. One of the most vivid memories I have from my early childhood is a time where my mother was away from the home for about three days and I, the firstborn, was left to care for my younger siblings. I was in charge. I made sure we took our baths and ate our meals. There was no babysitter, no father, and no supervision. This particular day I remember preparing a package of ramen noodles and peanut butter and jelly sandwiches. You'd be happy to know I've added a few more recipes to my chef list since then.

Because of these frequent unsupervised periods the State of Michigan eventually stepped in and removed us from my mothers home. Through this process we were separated into foster homes. I personally went through more than 20 different homes. I gave those foster parents a run for their money! They didn't know I would break windows and punch holes in the wall. In one home I even took the ladies purple nail polish and created a masterpiece on the bathroom wall.

Looking back I know that I was challenging each person to see if they would actually love me no matter what I did. I wanted to see how far could I push them before they would give up and send me to the next house. This left me searching for a real love, struggling with suicide and depression.

My adopted mother Martha Chatman had the courage to break through all of those walls. She was constantly correcting me, helping me to over-come the lies that I'd believed for myself. The best truth she shared with me is that Jesus loves me, and that he has a plan for my life. Those words should have provided comfort for me, but it only made me question. If God had a plan for my life wouldn't it make sense to create that plan while I was in my biological mother's home? Wouldn't it make sense to let me do that growing up with my real siblings?

Every morning at seven a.m. as Martha called us to the hallway outside our bedroom for bible study I was searching for this "plan for my life." Fast forward...I'm 21 years old, sitting at my desk working for a local insurance agency and I feel God's presence completely surround me in the middle of my work day. This is the day everything began to make sense, the day where purpose and destiny were born. I remember hearing this and grabbing the notepad on my desk to write down what I was feeling in my heart: *"My purpose is to remember my faith, and embrace my story, my flaws, and my successes, and use that to help children and parents going through foster care and adoption."* Suddenly tears started streaming from my eyes, and I knew that my past would not be the end of my story.

I believe that if you stay stuck trying to understand all the reasons why you'll miss the revelation. My story ended up serving as my platform to help broken people. God started moving in my life, opening doors for me to share what I'd been through. I was – and still am - in awe that he would use me to make a impact. I proudly defy all statistics that say because of the way I grew up and the neighborhood I lived in, that I would be less likely to be successful, or graduate high school, or that I would be unemployed and living from state provided funds. I am actively involved and invested in my community, assisting with mentoring programs, and speaking in front of thousands of young adults providing a message of hope and inspiration. Listen, God has a plan for you, a purpose that's revealed along the journey, I am living proof.

Mark often speaks at churches and youth conferences, sharing the hope he found in Christ whenever he gets the chance. He also expresses his hope and self worth through clothing and works at GoodBoy Clothing. You can find him and follow him on Instagram (@MarveousMark) and Face-Book (facebook.com/Mr.Chatman).

GINGER'S STORY

What are your future plans? It's difficult to find a junior in high school that hasn't been asked this question. But it was even harder for me as a junior in high school to have an answer. I spent the majority of my junior year bouncing from the idea of one major to the next, trying to figure out what God was calling me to pursue after high school. Physical therapy was a strong front-runner until I discovered I could not have a medical conversation without feeling queasy. I dabbled in the idea of dietetics, but then quickly decided I needed to give up the medical field altogether.

About a month after that decision, I began developing a passion for education. Throughout this entire process I had seen two career specialists who were working to help match me with the perfect career. Because of my interest in education they suggested that I interview a few of my teachers to find out what pros and cons they saw in their vocation. I wasn't expecting them to discourage me from pursuing a career in education, although I appreciated their honesty. So it was back to square one. This process continued throughout the course of my junior year- I would find a career I was excited and passionate about, but over time I would either watch that passion fade away or I would receive some sort of confirmation that I was pursuing the wrong career.

The pressure of trying to discern my next steps became a catalyst for a lot of stress and anxiety during that year of my life. It got to the point where anytime my mom brought up college or graduation, I shut myself off from the conversation completely. I avoided those conversations the best I could. That is how my junior year ended. I went into the summer feeling confused and stressed, with little direction for my future.

Even though school was out for the summer, the pressure and stress did not takie a vacation. However, like every summer, I went to church camp for a week with my youth group and God had

something special to tell me that week. The last day
of camp I had a conversation with my pastor and I
felt like I was supposed to ask him about his call to
ministry. What I have yet to mention is that I felt
God calling me to vocational ministry all the way
back in eighth grade. However, at that point in my
life I carried a lot of self-doubt and insecurity that
caused me to doubt God. I put my own limits on
God; deciding through my limited understanding
that God could not use me in ministry. I was
choosing to base my qualifications for ministry on
my personal doubts and flaws, instead of leaning in
and trusting on the true Qualifier.

My answer was no. So for three years I ran from
that calling, believing I could figure things out on
my own. Anytime the Holy Spirit resurfaced that
calling, I would just shove it back down. But something in my heart and mind changed that last day
of camp. I realized I had been holding on to an
anchor of self-reliance and fear, but God was asking
me to trade it in for the anchor of Christ. I knew
this meant entering into ministry and fully trusting
that God would bring fruition through it.

Since I have said yes to the call to ministry, God
has given me two great affirmations. The first was
an overwhelming sense of peace when I began

telling my family and friends that I was feeling lead to ministry - a peace that so immensely contrasted the stress I had felt all year. The second affirmation has been a growing passion for ministry. As I get further into my youth ministry courses at school, I have this growing sense of desire to serve God in this way and I have a growing assurance that this is the lifetime vocation He has set out for me.

I am currently reading a book entitled, "Strengthening the Soul of Your Leadership" by Ruth Haley Barton. In her book Barton writes, *"Our transformation is never for ourselves alone. It is always for the sake of others."* It is difficult to know exactly how the story of my struggle is helping others, but believing in the power of God assures me that He is using it to further His kingdom. My hope is that when you read this, you know that you are not alone. You are not alone in feeling anxious about the future. You are not alone in running from the calling God has given to you. You are not alone in feeling like you are not good enough. And, you are never out of reach from God. You are never too anxious for His indescribable peace to find you. You can never run far enough that God is not there. You were never meant to put your identity in the not-good-enough's.

In the midst of whatever struggle we face in this life, we are already more than conquerors through Christ. Final defeat can only overcome us when God's love can no longer reach us, but Scripture assures us that there is absolutely nothing and there is absolutely no one that can separate us from the love of God. A life in Christ gives us the capacity to claim a crushing victory over the obstacles that come our way. Satan wants nothing more than to see us doubt and run from God, but as followers of Christ we can have the confidence to know that through the darkest valleys God is with us. Not only did I find a calling and purpose through my struggle, but I experienced a God who said 'I am going to give you a victory that goes above and beyond anything you could have ever imagined for yourself.' What a gift it has been to participate in the overwhelming, eternal victory of Christ. God is inviting you to share in this victory too!

Ginger is currently studying Youth Ministry and Christian Education at Indiana Wesleyan University where she continues to walk faithfully in God's plan for her life. If you'd like to get in touch with her, you can send her an email at vlwhite33@yahoo.com

KRISTI'S STORY

Proverbs 4:23 – Above all else guard your
heart for everything you do flows
from it.

Many are familiar with this well-known scripture, but I find it most often applied in terms of dating for singles. I'd like to give another perspective on what it means to truly guard your heart, and why this scripture is imperative to your specific purpose and God given destiny. See I don't know about you- but after many years of stumbling around in the dark, I realized I did not want the pain of my past shaping the course of my future. In a generation that is burdened with young people growing up significantly impacted by darkness and pain, misguided and missing out on the abundant life in Christ at an alarming rate – I invite you to take a walk with me into the depth of my younger heart to see how unresolved pain altered the course of my life, but how the Lord stepped in to heal, restore and redirect my broken heart and mistakes for His good.

I vividly remember lying on the cold, dark basement floor, locked in a bathroom with a pillow and a couple squares of toilet paper to wipe away the endless flow of tears. I crawled into the laundry basket in a cupboard where I kept a small blanket to cling to after my father finished beating me physically and verbally in his fits of rage. That's where my shattered soul often cried myself to sleep. That night, as a young emotionally empty seven-year-old I cried out to a God, who I wasn't quite sure existed, and I begged Him to take me to Heaven. Surely if Heaven existed it had to be better than the life I endured in this place called "home". You see by seven years old I had already experienced abandonment by a mother I never met, a foster home, and adoption - followed by physical, verbal and emotional abuse from this "forever family." There is very little more damaging than a child growing up without love, acceptance and nurture. My body healed from the physical effects of scrapes, bloody noses, black eyes and bruises, but it was my broken spirit that caused years of setbacks, challenges and one bad decision after another.

I'm unlovable, no one will ever want me, even my own mom gave me away, I'm too difficult, I deserve this abuse because I'm just too hard to love. Those were the lies etched in my soul, subconsciously reverberating through my mind over the years. All my heart knew was pain and rejection, while all it desperately craved was love and acceptance. On the outside I radiated a false sense of confidence and pride with an identity built up in sports and successful accomplishments. I excelled in almost everything, but success only masked the layers of pain that had built a stone-cold barrier around my heart. The only thing I truly believed could be any better was death - to simply escape it all.

Yet, just as vividly as I recalled this memory – that night I heard a gentle, loving, warm voice whisper, *No. Daughter, I'm so sorry this is happening to you, but I have a plan and a purpose for you beyond anything your heart can imagine…..and while all you can see in this moment is the pain and darkness surrounding you I see the good that will become of it. Hold onto my voice through this journey and never let it go. I love you so much. You are very special to me. Daughter, I knit you together in your mother's womb. Every detail of your being I intricately created, and there is no one else like you in all the world. I will never leave you. I will always be with you, and I promise to protect you. So be strong and courageous sweet girl. No matter what, don't ever give up - for whatever you do and wherever you go I will be with you.*

This was the first memory I had of who God really was. How He chose me (John 15:16) before I ever chose Him. How God's love and grace relentlessly pursued me to redirect my life through every misstep. Even when the unresolved pain in my heart continued to take control. As I searched for love in all the wrong places and allowed my unguarded heart to guide the course of my life - by 21 I had a miscarriage, an abortion and two children out of wedlock. I quickly saw my dreams for law school with a family and the white picket fence fade as it was replaced with the struggle and reality of becoming a single parent.

I encountered this spiritual tug of war between the purpose and promises God had for me – who He created me to be and my reality of who I had become in this moment. I was overwhelmed by

shame and condemnation, and guilt for the life I
was creating for my own children. Yet, from that
very young age the Lord constantly reminded me of
my life scripture Joshua 1:6-9 *You must be strong and
courageous. Be brave. You must lead these people to inherit
their land that I promised.* Maybe that night God told
me to hold on because He knew what He could do
in this very moment when I began to give my life
unconditionally to Him. As I let God's grace wash
away every hidden trace of shame, as I listened and
received His truth about me to replace all the ugly
lies I previously believed and as I allowed His
perfect love to heal the depth of my broken soul I
began to find complete freedom in the love and life
of Jesus. As I received more of God's love and
forgiveness I began to extend the same love and
forgiveness to those that hurt me. In this journey,
God reminded me that He could take my old stony
heart and replace it with His heart of flesh giving
me His Spirit to guide the course of my life instead
of the pain (Ezekiel 36:26).

God began to use my pain and my story to
connect with others who found freedom and hope
in a vulnerable life with a similar story set free and
saved by God's everlasting grace. A passion began
to burn in my soul to share this story of redemption

through speaking, writing and teaching others how to let God restore our hearts, our relationships and our future. When I speak at events and people share that some part of my story saved their life or how they felt the love and grace of God like they never experienced before – I know that every part of my story was worth it. When I look back I realize there are so many times I could have lost my life, taken it or easily become a statistic. Instead, on the darkest days I knew from that very moment in that cold, sterile bathroom I made it, because I am, I was and I will always be more than a conqueror, and so are you.

I am convinced that God will use your greatest pain for His purpose and for your destiny. I don't believe you're reading this book by mistake. I believe God has a specific plan and a purpose for you too. Regardless of your choices, regardless of your past, regardless of where you find yourself in this very moment I invite you to receive God's love and give Him the unresolved pain in your heart. Let His grace overwhelm you, His Spirit guide you, and allow Him to use every piece of your pain and your story for His good.

Kristi currently enjoys raising her daughters in Dallas while pursuing one of her greatest passions – speaking, teach-

ing, writing, and encouraging others to live in the freedom and purpose God has uniquely called each one of us to – regardless of past or current circumstances. You can contact Kristi at the following email address: speakerauthorkristi-marie@gmail.com, or find her on FaceBook as Kristi Marie.

KIRK'S STORY

I'm sure I'm not the first small town guy to have a big dream. This dream was born for me in the summer of 2004. My faith in God was sky high at the time and my life was beyond full. I loved my church, our youth group was thriving, and I had amazing friends and a tremendous family. I had endless support as I began my high school years.

Before school started there was a conference in Phoenix, Arizona called Life 2004. It would be four days of powerful encounters with God, top-notch worship music, life-giving sermons, and on top of that, some of my favorite artists were going to be there. I'd been looking forward to Life 2004 with great anticipation, and finally the day came. My experience was nothing less than amazing. God showed up, and I was changed. So many of my friends were there and they all experienced God too. At the end of the conference, I felt like God was telling me that I was supposed to do ministry for His Kingdom. This was a pivotal point in my life and I was totally convinced that God had been preparing me for full time ministry for longer than I'd realized.

However, one of my favorite artists played at the conference and they happened to have a DJ spinning in the background. My heart started pounding and all I could think about was, "Could I ever spin records like that?" It looked so fun and exciting, and to be able to do it in a church setting was something I didn't know I wanted to do until I saw it. I knew I had to get a set of turntables as soon as I got back home.

After the conference ended, it was back to small town life in a rural town along the eastern edge of Montana. I approached my parents with the idea to let me purchase my first setup. I never had big plans beyond just doing it for fun. Sure I may have had crazy dreams that someday I'd be a DJ for a living, but never actually thought more beyond that in terms of putting together an action plan. I didn't believe God was interested in crazy dreams; only dreams that seemed "normal." In my eyes, chasing a dream of being a DJ full time was more of an irresponsible thing.

It would have to be a very "safe" risk if I ever was going to do it full time.

My "responsible" plan was to go to Crown College in Saint Bonifacious, MN, get my undergraduate degree, and then go on to work in youth ministry. But when scholarship money didn't come through, I was forced to look at alternative options. I'd actually played a bit of trumpet in high school and because of that, Dickinson State University offered me a music scholarship. I accepted. I didn't see it at the time, but God was using the music classes I was enrolled in to teach me things I would use later. I was thinking Dickinson was just a place where I could get my generals done, and move on to pursuing youth ministry at a Bible college.

However, one class in public speaking changed everything for me. I found a new passion there and ended up graduating with my B.A. degree in Communications.

After I finished college, I got a good job in sales, and I thought I had a perfect plan. I would work hard, get married, buy a home, start a family, raise kids, and retire with the same company at an early age. I thought I was living the good life. Then one day, things changed abruptly. If you're ever around people who are followers of Christ, you might hear them say that God closes doors that no one else can open and opens doors that no one else can close. It's actually in the Bible! (Revelation 3:7, paraphrase mine) I'll tell you, God began to close some doors in my life. Opportunities that once seemed so amazing and perfect suddenly became questionable. My once crystal clear plans for the future suddenly became clouded with uncertainty. I can't explain the exact details or tell you precisely how it all happened, but I know that God was working in my life. He was redirecting my steps, and something in me started wondering if there was more for me than this job in sales. This question of, "what if?" haunted me and I couldn't stop wondering if my dreams of being a DJ full time could come true, and if God could somehow use this as a ministry.

As my plans crumbled around me I had a moment of clarity. I had no idea what would happen with my job, but I knew I couldn't ignore this desire to pursue DJ-ing any longer. No longer would I play it safe. I was finally going to be one of those guys who actually pursued his dreams! I wasn't going to sit on the sidelines working a job with an uncertain future while I saw people all around me answering the call to follow their dreams.

So once again I had a plan! But God had a ton of work to do in my character to get me to the place where I could actually handle what He wanted to give me.

I'll be the first to admit that I was obsessed with my bank account. Quitting my job meant I would have to live off of less money while I figured out how to support my dream. While I had some savings, I knew I would need to supplement my income somehow so I applied for several jobs. I really thought God was calling me to pursue this dream. And surely He would know I'd need money to make it a reality, but no one was returning my calls. Day after day there were no responses. No interviews, no options, and I had no idea what to do. I started questioning God. I wondered why God made the promise that He would provide, yet no opportunities were coming in after all these phone calls and emails. It didn't make sense. Did God lie about his promise? What was I missing? I started to actually think God was the source of my problems. I had no idea that He wanted to give me something more than just money. He wanted to deliver me from the way I thought about money, and set me free from the love of money that had crept into my life so gradually.

You see, I had always equated my identity with how much money I had. I used to think that the size of my bank account determined my self worth. God's plan for me through all of this was to grow my character to the point where I realized that He alone is the one true source of my identity and worth. I could be the richest guy on the planet, or not have a single dime to my name – and neither of those things would change how much God loves me and values me. As God was bringing about this change in my character through the circumstances of my life, he brought a man into my life at a pivotal moment.

I met Dave at church, which I believe was an act of divine intervention. God knew I would need someone to walk with me while He chiseled away at some of my character flaws as I kept kicking and screaming. I was never good at embracing change when God wanted to change me. I used to fight against it.

Helplessly I watched as my bank account shrank each month, despite my best efforts to make progress financially. It seemed like no matter what I did, I just kept losing money. I was trying hard to get DJ gigs, but nothing was materializing. Dave walked through this confusing time with me, helping me to move from trusting in people's opinions to trusting the living God of the universe. Because of his guidance and counsel, I was able to grow and learn about trusting God in the dark times. In 2014, I was looking forward to better times as I had decided to move to Minneapolis, MN to continue my pursuit of being a DJ in ministry. I signed with a record label in the cities and was excited for the opportunities to come! I thought after all the struggles and all the failure, this would finally be my big break and God was coming through for me.

Unfortunately, the opportunity never materialized. Disappointment, discouragement, and confusion set in once again. At this point, I was so close to giving up. In my mind, I had served my rough year of trials; I was not ready or willing to go through any more character building circumstances. I thought God owed it to me to bring a silver lining to my troubles. However, there was no silver lining in sight. False hope, cancelled gigs, and an abundance of turmoil within the company lead to me asking God if it was worth it to stay the course.

I remember vividly making threats at God, as if I could twist his arm with my ill-tempered coercion. I vowed, "Lord, if you leave me hanging out here in northern Minnesota, I will devote myself to all the pleasure I can find." Every night before I fell asleep, it was as if these threats kept replaying in my mind, almost as if to say, "What are you going to do now, God?" I knew that following this path wouldn't bring me fulfillment, but at the same time, I wanted release from the despair I felt.

By God's grace alone, I stayed committed to the Lord's plan and bought out of my deal with the recording label in 2015. At this point, I had nearly exhausted all my savings and had no clue how people were going to start saying yes instead of no. I remember driving home from working out one afternoon when the Lord put an impression on my heart saying, "You won't have to go find another job." Could this really be God or was I delusional by now? I committed to making as many phone calls in the months to come. I traveled a lot of miles. It didn't necessarily look like I had always imagined traveling as a DJ. Driving ten to twelve hours for gigs back home isn't necessarily a sign of success in the industry. But at the time it was all I had and was thankful for every gig. I knew I needed to start somewhere.

Sometimes just starting – just taking a few steps, with a right heart, is all it takes. One step after another, I slowly but surely found the path that God had for me. It was in no way overnight success. But it is a story of God's never ending provision. Various opportunities came, and I showed up. And God gave me the chance to showcase myself as a DJ, which allowed me to eventually establish myself as a DJ. I am not ashamed to say that in 2015 I had made enough income to continue living my dreams; in 2016, God had doubled my income from the previous year! I have released two EPs in the past two years, one of which recently released on 4/28/17. That album reached #31 on the iTunes top dance charts in the US…. I am a living testimony to God's grace, provision, and sovereignty.

Was it easy? No. Was it confusing? More than you know! But did I give up? Never. If you have a dream, chase it. Let God purify your heart so that your character can sustain you in the places He desires to bring you. It might be a longer process that you want, with twists and turns and losses along the way, but God has a plan for you. And He is able to do exceedingly, abundantly, above and beyond all that we could ask or think! (Ephesians 3:20)

DJ Kirk is now touring full time with his latest record debuting #33 on the Top 200. He would love to come perform at your next convention or youth rally. More info can be found at www.iamdjkirk.com.

CAITLIN'S STORY

I was fourteen when I met him. He told his mom that day he wondered if he would marry me. He was cute, fun and hey – he was a great soccer player! Four days later we spent hours sitting on the swings alone in his backyard with no lulls in the conversation. We became instant best friends. We spent three years building a relationship long distance and when I was seventeen when I moved to be near him. We were so excited about our future together. Sounds like the back story of a romantic movie doesn't it?

While I thought we talked about everything, he'd been hiding an addiction that started at age 13 – a sexual addiction that stemmed from a traumatic event in his childhood that I knew nothing about. It was a lot harder for him to hide his acting out cycles when I lived nearby. I caught glimpses of his impulsive behaviors but didn't understand the root causes and deep wounds it was creating by ignoring his behavior and making light of it. I believed if our circumstances changed he would change.

I was twenty when we got married. I had no idea until the day we got married that I had already closed my heart off. It was painfully obvious from the start that this wasn't the way marriage was supposed to be. There had already been too much betrayal for me to push through and be open with him. I spent seven years wondering what was wrong with me, seven years thinking I was the problem, seven years ignoring the obvious signs that it wasn't just me.

The day life came crashing down because he fed his addiction to the point of causing legal intervention was the day I turned 28. It was July 9th - my birthday. We were getting ready to go out to dinner. Our daughter was 16 months old and we were five weeks pregnant with baby number two! It should have been an exciting day, but instead the police showed up. When they left a few minutes later with him, I sat there on the stairs clinging to my daughter. I knew that life would never be the same. The following months were filled with numbness, morning sickness, tears, darkness and a lot of broken dreams. I thought God was crazy. Didn't he know I was about to become a single mom? Didn't he know what my husband was doing? Didn't God know he would be arrested? Why did he give me another baby now?

There was so much guilt, shame and fear that surrounded me. What I expected my life to be like was completely torn out from underneath me. I felt so inadequate to be a mom to two little girls. How could one parent ever be enough for two precious lives? It seemed that the losses were never ending. It created severe brokenness in our friendships, our family, and our church. It affected our income, our future plans and our children deeply. There have been times where it seemed that every single aspect of my life was marred by his sin and my emotional distance. I still experience loss because of this in ways I can't foresee until it arrives.

I had experienced hard loss before. My mom died when I was twenty-one and I closed myself off. I had shut my emotions off within my marriage, but after my mom died I decided I was done with being hurt and I didn't want to be close to anyone – friends, family, God. So I became a shell. I went through my days doing what I needed to. I enjoyed my friendships on a shallow level and had plenty of fun but buried my emotions deep and did my best to never really feel anything, good or bad. But with all my effort to protect myself I ended up in a place so dark I realized that it is better to have joy and sorrow than just sorrow. Brene Brown says "Numb the dark and you numb the light." I had never understood that before. So after he was arrested I ran hard towards God. I ran deep into my friendships and made vulnerability a priority in my life. I soaked in God's promise of Isaiah 43 every day. No matter how dark the night, how unable I felt to move forward, I knew that the waves of grief would not overtake me. I rested in the fact that His love is perfect and steadfast, unlike any human can give me. I looked up every reference to his steadfast love. I looked up every time in the Bible that it said, "do not fear" to see *why* God says do not fear – it is because of who He is! I studied God's faithfulness to the unfaithful Israelites and I chose to trust in that love, one that is constant and will not waver.

There were days I would talk to myself and tell myself to just breath, to get up and feed the kids, to reach out for help. While there is a necessary period of paralyzation when life falls apart, when it lasts too long we begin to wound our loved ones by not being present, by waiting to be rescued, by not really living. I was determined to not just survive. I wanted something better than that for my two girls. I didn't want them to look back and remember me as the mom who just survived the pain. I want them to see a woman who chose joy, chose love, and chose hope. I want them to see that in Jesus they can find a love that will never let them down.

Three years later I am so thankful that I have taken many steps towards being the woman I want my girls to look back on and say, "she thrived!" I would not be nearly as independent, joyful and grateful for where I am without the amazing support of my church body and friends. There are still days where I want to give up and just wallow in sorrow when I realize another loss I hadn't experienced before, relive hard memories or just am tired of doing life as a single parent. But one thing a lot of people don't realize is that joyfulness and thankfulness is a choice. I could easily be a bitter and depressed single mom, having to work and put my kids in daycare and not live life as I planned. Or I can choose to be grateful for the blessings that pop up all over in my life and decide to create joy in my life. My attitude is what I choose for it to be, and that attitude shapes the

course of my day and the environment I set for
my girls.

I have learned much about God and about
myself over these few years. It has been fun to
revive my personality and find things to do that
bring me joy. It is worth the vulnerability with
others to sometimes have my heart feel raw. I have
learned that church is for messy people, not seem-
ingly put together hypocrites. I have already seen
God use my brokenness to give others hope and I
am eager to be used in substantial ways in the
future to help others find healing. It is the course of
life to have painful events and I am honored every
time someone reaches out to me to me from their
own pain to ask me for a glimmer of hope. I aim to
be the moonlight in their night and give them the
hope that God will take their shattered heart and
make their life a beautiful mosaic.

Isaiah 63:1-3 *"The Spirit of the Sovereign Lord is on
me, because the Lord has anointed me to proclaim good news
to the poor. He has sent me to bind up the brokenhearted, to
proclaim freedom for the captives and release from darkness for
the prisoners, to proclaim the year of the Lord's favor and the
day of vengeance of our God, to comfort all who mourn, and
provide for those who grieve in Zion— to bestow on them a
crown of beauty instead of ashes, the oil of joy instead of*

mourning, and a garment of praise instead of a spirit of despair."

Caitlin is currently enjoying being a mom, a manager at her work, and a hope giver to those in her life. She is eager to be used further in ways that bring hope and healing to others. You can reach her at caitlinmwaldron@gmail.com or find her on FaceBook as Caitlin Miller Waldron.

SHEILA'S STORY

2013 was the year that would change my life forever. Ever since our second son came into the world in 2010, my heart longed for one more baby. My husband thought I was completely nuts because of how severely ill I become during my pregnancies. Before I ever missed a period or needed to look at a calendar, I'd be puking my guts out, already knowing I was pregnant and the next nine months would be complete hell. Despite the fact that my first and second pregnancies had been difficult the entire nine months, I felt strongly that "third time's a charm, right?" Wrong!

Sure enough, my third pregnancy was no different. Immediately I began questioning why God would allow this for the third time. On top of the horrible fatigue, "morning sickness" that lasted all day and all night, and having two other toddlers to try and cope with, my dad was diagnosed with multiple myeloma, an incurable cancer of the blood. All of this felt like too much to bear.

After several emotional conversations with God, desperately seeking advice from friends, attempting chemotherapy medication for the third time for nausea, and even giving hypnotherapy a valid shot, I began working with a nutritionist to try and relieve some of my symptoms. I was literally willing to do anything that would help me feel better. I so desperately wanted to have just one pregnancy that I could enjoy. After detoxing my body for five days and barely hanging on at 97 pounds, I was determined to get better. My nutritionist placed me on a very strict eating schedule with little room for grace. In the past it had taken about 20 weeks or so before I had started to feel better. This time, however, was better. I was starting to feel hopeful around 12 weeks pregnant.

Unfortunately, just as I was starting to feel better, my dad took a turn for the worse. There was nothing we could do but pray. That summer, my dad had to undergo "super chemotherapy" and a stem cell transplant at the Mayo Clinic in Rochester, Minnesota. My parents moved to Rochester for the summer, and, praise Jesus, my dad survived. My mom, like an angel by his side, has always been there to take care of and show love to our family. I am so blessed by her!

They returned home at the end of August and a week later, on September 5th, our third baby boy was born. He was as beautiful and precious as our other two boys. As expected, the first month was a little fuzzy. Going on little sleep, running to soccer games and trying to keep up with three children, all while nursing and getting back to a somewhat normal diet was exhausting!

The last Sunday in September was a day I will never forget. We celebrated our second son's 3rd birthday with our whole family. It was a good day, but I wasn't prepared for what the week ahead would entail. That night, I didn't sleep. I was way beyond tired, but I could not fall asleep. The next night, I did not sleep once again. The following night, I wouldn't sleep again. That Thursday, it was my birthday. All I truly wanted, by that point, was to fall asleep. I needed it so desperately! I told my husband that it was the worst birthday I had ever had in my life and he said, "Then next year will be the best." Oh, how I prayed that he would be right.

That night, I didn't sleep again. The next morning, it was critical that I see my doctor. He prescribed some medications and told my husband to let me sleep all weekend while he took care of the family. We left the clinic thinking once I had some sleep that weekend, this would all be over by Monday. We had no idea how difficult the battle would be!

Beyond desperate for sleep, I took my medication and went to my son's room with great anticipation to sleep until whenever I woke up. It was so disheartening to wake up an hour or two later. I could not believe this was happening! I could not understand it at all. I was in a complete panic. By early Sunday morning, I was crawling out of my skin. I was begging God to help me sleep, just for a few hours.

That day, I was admitted to the hospital. Waiting in the emergency room, I begged them to sedate me because I was in so much mental and emotional pain, but they wanted to wait until evening. As I lay in that hospital bed, all alone, I knew what it felt like to want to die. I could empathize with someone who wanted to commit suicide because that was exactly what I felt at that moment. I wanted to die. Not because I didn't love my family or my newborn baby, but in that very moment, after not sleeping for more than a couple of hours for an entire week, it hurt to be in my body. I just wanted out of my mind. I held on, barely, until evening. I have no idea what pill they gave me that night, but I couldn't wait to take it! What seemed like an hour later, I woke in another panic. The nurses rushed in and stuck a needle in my arm. Finally. I was going to sleep.

The next morning I was still extremely tired, my mind still racing. I knew I could not go home with whatever drug they put in my arm. So, we would try something different that night. Another sleepless night. By Wednesday morning, I woke to the sun shining in my hospital room and it had been the first time I had slept, without interruption, in ten days. I told the doctor that whatever pill I had been given the night before, I would not be going home without it. I also had an appointment set up for a month out with a psychiatrist, but I knew that if I was going to stay alive, I had to have that appointment immediately.

Thank the Lord, I was able to get my appointment moved up to the following day. I was released from the hospital that afternoon. I was terrified. My body was frantic. My mind was spinning. I have never been so afraid in my entire life.

The next day, my husband took me to meet my psychologist and psychiatrist. I was prescribed some heavy medication. It didn't faze me one bit. I just knew I needed to trust the doctors God had brought to me and listen to their words of wisdom and trust the process. But every time someone said, "process," I was even more panicked. I didn't want this to be a process. I wanted it to be over as soon as possible.

My psychiatrist informed me that in order for my brain to begin to heal, I would need to sleep in a room by myself for the next several months, away from my husband and baby so that my sleep would not be interrupted. During my hospital stay, I had to wean from nursing due to short and long-term medications, and now I had to be quarantined at night? Just when I thought things should start getting better, they were only getting worse. I felt like motherhood was being completely ripped away from me. It felt like I was being tortured and I had no idea why. During my pregnancy, I longed to have the same wonderful bond like I had with my second son. I was so grateful for it because I did not have that with my first. It was all being taken away so suddenly without my control, without my consent, and there was nothing I could do about it. This made it even more devastating. I then fell into several months of deep, dark, and terrifying depression and anxiety.

Every night we'd put the older boys to bed and then my dear husband would get up twice each night with the baby and then go to work the next day, while I was "banished" to a different room in our home to sleep. Walking downstairs to the dark and lonely room that would be my bedroom for the next few months felt like I was walking down to hell every night. I had two hours before I could take my sleeping pill. Two hours felt like eternity! The house was dead quiet and I was left all alone with my crazy thoughts. If you have ever experienced extreme anxiety, you may know what I'm talking about. My mind could not focus on anything - not television, computers, phones - even very simple decision-making was very difficult for me at that point. All I could do was pray. I would fall to my knees in tears and plead with God to heal me, to save my family from this. He felt so distant during this time, but my mom assured me that He was hearing every word! Even though I would take a sleep medication every night, the anxiety made me feel like I would not sleep if I didn't recite Philippians 4:6-13 before I could fall asleep.

"Don't worry about anything, but pray about everything. With thankful hearts offer up your prayers and requests to God. Then, because you belong to Christ Jesus, God will bless you with peace that no one can completely understand. And this peace will control the way you think and feel. Finally, my friends, keep your minds on whatever is true, pure, right, holy, friendly, and proper. Don't ever stop thinking about what is truly worthwhile and worthy of praise. You know the teachings I gave you, and you know what you heard me say and saw me do. So follow my example. And God, who gives you peace, will be with you. The Lord has made me very grateful that at last you have thought about me once again. Actually, you were thinking about me all along, but you didn't have any chance to show it. I am not complaining about having too little. I have learned to be satisfied with whatever I have. I know what it is to be poor or to have plenty, and I have lived under all kinds of conditions. I know what it means to be full or to be hungry, to have too much or too little. Christ gives me the strength to face anything." (Philippians 4:6-13 CEV)

It's easy to read and recite that, but to truly trust and believe it when you are walking a very scary road are two completely different things. I had to go through the motions because I do know that God is always good and has our best interest at heart. God was providing even when we felt like we were living in "survival mode" for so long. We had so much support. Friends from church and small groups came to bring meals and pray with us. Family came to help as well. Every afternoon I needed to call my best friend just to hear her say, "You will get better, I promise!" I wanted to believe that, but week after week with little change, we were losing hope. She said, "I wish I could show you a video of your family in 5 years from now and show you how happy you are." I hung onto that. I clung to the things that brought some comfort, especially Scripture.

As the calendar turned to 2014, I made a promise to God. I told Him, "I cannot go through another year like this! I can't be the wife or mother I desire to be. If You heal me, I promise to serve You for the rest of my life. I surrender it all to You!"

Let me tell you, He heard every word. Every tear, He heard as a prayer. I cannot describe the trauma my family and I suffered during this time. But God, in all of His sovereignty, needed my attention. He chose me. He wanted all of me. I now understand that He was answering so many of my prayers from years before. I needed to go through this to get there.

Since then, I am healed. I am continually being made whole. I cannot explain the peace and joy that He has brought me. I look at life differently. I empathize intensely. I will never take life for granted again! I can now look back on that season with kindness, knowing He was pursuing me desperately. Our basement is like our own personal "war room" and the place I began painting beauty from ashes. God has given me my business ministry. He has shown me that when we pray, we can "expect Him to answer us, and tell us great and mighty things which we did not know." (Jeremiah 33:3)

These days I have the great honor and privilege of designing and creating inspirational custom apparel and jewelry. "Great and mighty things" that I never would have been able to do if I was still in control of my own life. He blows my mind daily! I not only believe in the power of prayer, but God truly does "work ALL things together for good, to those who love Him and are called according to His purpose." (Romans 8:28)

We are all called. We are all chosen. We all have a story. This is just the beginning of mine.

#PRAYMOHR®

If you need prayer, please reach out to Sheila at Face-book.com/PRAYMOHR

She is online to pray and encourage you through whatever trial you may be facing. You are never alone!

ABOUT THE AUTHOR

For More Information:

www.PorciaBaxter.com